# ON
# TROUBLESOME
# CREEK

# ON TROUBLESOME CREEK

A true story about Christian
service in the mountains of Kentucky

Melodie M. Davis

HERALD PRESS
Scottdale, Pennsylvania
Kitchener, Ontario
1983

Library of Congress Cataloging in Publication Data

Davis, Melodie M., 1951-
   On Troublesome Creek.

   Summary: The author's account of her experiences as
a Mennonite voluntary service worker in a small, poverty-
stricken Appalachian mining community in Kentucky.
      1. Davis, Melodie M., 1951-      2. Volunteer
workers in social service—Kentucky—Biography.
3. Christian life—Mennonite authors.   4. Appalachian
Region—Social conditions. [1.   Davis, Melodie M.,
1951-   .   2. Volunteer workers in social service.
3. Christian life.   4. Mennonites.   5. Appalachian
Region—Social conditions.   6. Kentucky—Social
conditions]   I. Title.
HV98.K4D38   1983      361.7'5'0924 [B] [92]      83-18541
ISBN 0-8361-3347-1 (pbk.)

ON TROUBLESOME CREEK
Copyright © 1983 by Herald Press, Scottdale, Pa.  15683
   Published simultaneously in Canada by Herald Press,
   Kitchener, Ont.  N2G 4M5
Library of Congress Catalog Card Number: 83-18541
International Standard Book Number: 0-8361-3347-1
Printed in the United States of America
Design by Alice B. Shetler

83 84 85 86 87 88 10 9 8 7 6 5 4 3 2 1

Dedicated to my parents,
who nurtured my interest in
service, and who are practicing
what they preached!

# Contents

I have changed the names of some of the persons involved in my story to protect their privacy. In other cases names were changed just to avoid confusion between two characters with the same name. All persons are real, although not all conversations occurred exactly as I've written them, nor in the chronological order they appear in the book. But all conversations *are* faithful representations (as near as my memory and journal could recall) of actual conversations and my relationship to the characters.

—*Melodie M. Davis*

# Author's Preface

When I was a little girl, our family spent one summer vacation relieving the pastor of a small mountain Mennonite church in Appalachia. One of my most vivid memories is of being teased that a butch-haired, dirty, little Sunday school boy was madly in love with me.

Another memory is of a dusty afternoon drive up one of the winding mountain roads, to visit the small Talcum Mennonite Church. Our family photo album still sports a picture of four carefree children in front of that little clapboard church. Little did I know that I would one day return to that community and that church as a voluntary service worker.

I remember enjoying an overnight stay at a Hannibal, Missouri, unit on another family vacation, and then a work trip by our youth group to South Texas voluntary service units years later. I think it was this early and frequent exposure to voluntary service by my parents that made service attractive to me. While other girls envisioned themselves as nurses, mothers, or teachers, I guess I pictured myself in a unit: singing around the piano, washing dishes together, leading worship at church.

But real life in a voluntary service unit had little of that romance. It was simply life in all its ordinariness, albeit with rainbows. This first came as a shock and then I gradually realized that this was as it should be: voluntary service is not something to do just for a year or two, but is a good way to start a lifestyle.

And that is my purpose in writing this book: to highlight the normal ups and downs of life as a voluntary service worker—the failures, the too few successes, the commitment, the mixed motives, the groping for further direction for life. I hope that those who have had similar experiences will be enabled to reflect and work through some of their own conflicting emotions. I hope that this book will encourage young people who have thought, "Maybe sometime I'll go into voluntary service," to go out and *do* it!

I want this book to capture a period of history and color in Appalachia which may soon be gone forever because of acculturization and "progress." I want to portray a realistic-as-possible picture of life in a voluntary service unit: the good, the bad, the indifferent. I want to take the reader inside a young girl's mind and heart in her first year away from home, as she flirts with love and its illusions, and as she agonizes over which way next.

This book is for anyone who was ever young, idealistic, and attempting to find "God's will." It's also for anyone who has ever fallen in love with a special part of the country, a people, and perhaps even a special person—only to be faced with the bittersweet task of needing to move on.

—*Melodie M. Davis*
Harrisonburg, Virginia

# On Troublesome Creek

# What on earth am I doing on a Greyhound bus on a Friday night?

To look at me, I suppose I could have been one of thousands of teenagers who run away from home every year. Jeans, loose jacket, an odd collection of bags and boxes. Long brown hair—probably stringy after trying to sleep on a Greyhound.

And I probably even had that searching, hopeful, lost puppy dog look. It was 1970, during hippie love-ins, Jesus people, and all that.

But I wasn't running away from anything. I definitely had my parents' blessing to enter voluntary service. In fact, one of my father's favorite lines (along with "save your kisses for the man you marry") was, "It sure would make me happy if even just one of my kids went into voluntary service someday."

Suddenly I became aware that the man in the seat across

the aisle and one row up had turned and was appraising me with a lewd sneer.

I felt my cheeks flush. Perhaps one of my unvoiced reasons for going into voluntary service was to meet guys, but this really wasn't the kind of man I was hoping to meet. Especially not when I was all alone in a packed Greyhound bus somewhere between Indianapolis and Cincinnati.

I watched disinterestedly out the window. But he was not the type to be easily discouraged by a cold shoulder.

"Hey, beautiful. . . ." I felt his stare penetrate my facade of woman-of-the-world.

I knew that he knew I was all alone, and that I was probably a fresh country girl venturing out on my own for the first time. City people can always tell who the newcomers are. An unsure glance in several directions . . . a timid walk . . . a look of: "Now who's going to mug me?"

I could see that he was literally chain smoking, lighting one cigarette on the butt of another. His boldness grew. He placed a stained grubby hand on the seat right next to my leg. I was shaking inside, and glad I had chosen to wear jeans instead of the skirt I had almost put on.

"Please, mister," I said, daring really to look at him for the first time. His eyes were bloodshot and sick.

Even though the bus was nearly full, I spied one empty seat about three rows up. If I had only been more experienced I wouldn't have sat in the back of the bus in the first place.

I collected myself and my bags and staggered the few steps up the aisle to the welcome seat.

"So this is voluntary service," I mumbled as I eased into my seat.

A certain Nancy Drew spirit of adventure tingled inside me though. I was proud of myself for not panicking, for actually coping with a drunk man. And I was still a little scared of his next move.

I lost him in the desolate Cincinnati station, and lightheartedly boarded the bus bound for Hazard, Kentucky, via Lexington. Now a bonafide seasoned bus traveler, I perched myself in the very front row, and soon found myself caught up eavesdropping on a homespun conversation between the bus driver and one of his regular passengers on that route. They rambled as much as the bus did, about Mrs. Ritchie's arthritis and Uncle Ben's German shepherd. The bus twisted down hairpin curves, while the sun slid behind the mountains.

"What on earth am I doing on a Greyhound on a Friday night in September?" I pinched myself. "I ought to be in college, or at work, or on a date, or with a bunch of girls, or watching TV with my family." All of a sudden the world seemed very big and the mountains very lonely.

Frankly, I was one of many of the class of '70 who didn't know quite what to do with themselves. College was too "establishment." Getting a job in the hometown was too boring, providing there was even one to be found. I could have gotten married, I guess—but with that level of excitement about the prospect, it's probably lucky for him that I didn't take him up on it.

The guidance people had tried their best to counsel me to college—"Oh, you're perfect college material!" Whatever that was! Was I just a piece of dress material for some university to cut and sew according to a stamped, mass-produced pattern? I had a vague notion of things I'd maybe like to be, but nothing so definite as to be able to "declare a major," like you had to do if you went to college in those days. Besides, both of my sisters had gone straight from high school to college. I thought I had to do something different—after being stuck in hand-me-down dresses all my life.

Not very pure motives on which to begin a stint as a church volunteer, I'll admit. Of course, I had nobler goals to put on the application forms. I wanted to "help people." A lot of us wanted to save the world in those post-'60s days. Disillusioned with the selfishness of doing your own thing and letting it all hang out, many of us turned to saving the world. Never mind that the world didn't really want to be saved.

All cynicism aside, I *was* sincere: romantic, dedicated, eighteen, naive—and sincere.

I also dearly loved children. So I thought that my assignment as a nursery school teacher would be a creative challenge and good experience for future reference. I was also to work with 4-H clubs, teaching home economics skills to girls who supposedly hadn't been taught anything by their mothers.

I knew I would be living with other young people in a setup called a voluntary service (VS) unit. In my unit there would be one married couple (to make the living situation acceptable for parents), two unmarried guys, and one other unmarried girl. (We defined everyone in those preliberation days in terms of "married" or "unmarried.")

I knew that I would have to write my own job description to a certain extent, in a job for which I had virtually no preparation. I knew that I would be living in a strange culture with strange people and that I probably wouldn't see "home" for a whole year. It was exhilarating and at the same time, in my heart of hearts, a little awesome.

The bus was coming near the end of its line, and there were only a few other passengers left. It was completely dark and had started raining—making the night all the thicker. I could no longer make out the shape of the mountains—but because I knew they were still there, hiding, they seemed to close in on me all the more. An occasional splotch of light splashed from home windows high on the mountainsides. Sometimes I caught a glimpse here and there of mothers putting supper on tables, or of young girls playing piano by the living-room window.

I always like arriving at new places at night, for part of the surprise and mystery of a strange place is held captive by the night—to be revealed only next morning in fresh light. It is like saving some of your presents to open Christmas morning.

Lawrence and Judi Brenneman, the leaders of the voluntary service unit, were at the bus station to meet me about 11:30 p.m. The station was a crackerbox, a far cry from the bustle of the Cincinnati and Indianapolis stations. Suddenly the sick man on the Greyhound seemed days ago; my parents and the farm were light years removed. The fifteen-mile drive from Hazard to our unit home, above a store in the little post office town of Ary, passed in a blur of swishing windshield wipers, courteous questions as to where I came from and what my two weeks of orientation at the voluntary service headquarters had been like.

Judi quickly showed me where my bed and the bathroom were, with instructions to sleep as late as I wanted in the morning. There was a whole year in which I could explore my new home.

# 2

# The honeymoon

Coal trucks awakened me before the morning sun actually had a chance. About 5:00 a.m., I jolted, hearing a trucker shifting down through his gears to round the ninety-degree curve directly outside my window. The truck backfired, the brakes squawked, and then the trucker put down the pedal once again, to build back his speed. Our road was the route from the mining town out to the strip mines and back, and that morning serenade was soon to become only background noise.

After this initial rude awakening, I dozed on and off a few more hours since I was still exhausted from the trip the day before. Finally it was a respectable hour to get up.

I looked out the best I could from my bedroom window on the world. Here was the "gift" I had eagerly awaited the night before. To the east was the highway, running beside a dancing wide creek. The creek provided a constant roar, except when competing with coal trucks and jalopies. A mist blanketed the tops of the mountains beside the creek, so all I could actually see were dark, lush depths of green velvet: the woods and hills lining the babbling creek. I said its name softly to myself, "Troublesome Creek." The unit leader, Lawrence, had told me the name the night before. Just *one* of the colorful names these mountain people dubbed their landmarks. I wondered what was troublesome about it, and why it had garnered such a mischievous name.

It was going to be a pretty day, I was sure, since the night rains had cleansed the skies and mountains. I itched to climb and know the mountains—to know them as intimately as the pasture fields and woods of my father's farm. Someday I would, I promised myself.

I started to dress, for I could hear morning noises coming from the rest of the house and the store below. It was Saturday, a day "off" for most of the unit members.

So after breakfast, Judi took me on my very first visit to the store below our apartment. Rachel's store, as it was known, was one of those marvelous country varieties that still dot the hills (and plains, for that matter) of backside America. It was the place for everyone to stop at least once a day. Men stopped on their way to work at the strip mines to buy a pack of crackers and vienna sausages for lunch. Children dropped by after school for bubble gum, candy bars, potato chips, and "soda water." Wives came for a gallon of milk or eggs during the day. And on Saturdays whole families would clamber onto the back of the pickup and burrow out of the "hollers" (mountain valleys) to lay in supplies for a week or month. And after summer suppers, sunsets would paint the evening sky as men and boys played out their lives on the stage in front of the store: cars, girls, booze, work, and tobacco. The women were strangely absent from this nighttime arena, banished, I suppose, to be barefoot in the kitchen, or at least stringing beans on the front porch. The young men would gather by the "newest" car, usually a jalopy to you and me, but the lucky owner was converting it with stereo, speakers, decals, and a loud muffler, into a *real* car.

Rachel's store was actually tended by Rachel's bachelor son, Bert. It was a family enterprise, though. Sometimes loud, but good-natured, discussions came up through the floorboards to the unit apartment, over how to run the store.

You could buy almost anything in the store, from a dusty can of deodorant to good mellow hoop cheese. Most of the items lined high shelves behind a counter, and Bert retrieved them for customers. The prices were higher, of course, than in town, but if you had to drive fifteen miles to save a dime, conventional wisdom had it, it wasn't worth the drive to town. Sometimes a box of Sugar Crisp wasn't exactly crisp anymore, though.

Bert was mostly businesslike. It was as though he wanted you to know he was running a *real* business. But his wry, wrinkled face would crack into a toothy, self-conscious grin at times, too. If he didn't have an item that you needed right away for a special recipe you were in the middle of making, he could always "order it."

On my first trip down to the store with Judi, I felt like a monkey on parade. Several teenage boys lounged around the outside of the store. Conversations suddenly ceased. I smiled self-consciously, not knowing whether to say, "Hi," "How do you do," or not say anything at all. After Judi and I were safely in the store, we heard a low whistle. "Oh, you'll get used to that," Judi said reassuringly.

We met Bert, Rachel, and Goldie (who was Bert's sister). The store smelled of fresh bakery bread, stale meat, and hoop cheese. We asked Bert how he was today and would he get us a gallon of milk, please. Bert, puffing his pipe, half-limped to the back of the store and brought back a fresh carton. We were buying on credit, but there were no credit cards or little machines to worry about. Bert simply penciled the purchase into a notebook. Accounts were kept simply—not quite on the back of a hand, but almost. Most store-keepers in the hollows extended interest-free credit, even when they couldn't really afford it. The people wouldn't "trade" where the storekeeper became too "hard."

I took it all in like a little girl at a candy store. It seemed like a book or TV show, like I had wandered onto the set of a high school play.

In time, the friendly bang of the door in the morning as customers came and went was reassuring. It meant that all was well in the hollows nearby and on Troublesome Creek. It meant that the store hadn't closed for someone's funeral and that Bert was well. The store was a gathering point, a news center, a social hall, a courting place. And if all else failed, it was a place to buy bread.

After a weekend of polite introductions, I was only too glad to get down to "business" on Monday. After lunch, Lawrence took me to the little brown-brick schoolhouse across the creek from our apartment.

It was an elementary school, and the smells of my younger years came rushing back when we stepped inside the school doors. There was a musty mix of paste, after-dinner staleness from the cafeteria, dirt, and the sweat of children who'd played outside for three recesses and were clamoring to go home.

We met the eager principal who walked us through halls and up and down the stairs. At one door, a harried teacher came to tap Mr. Hollinger on the shoulder in a plea for help. Through smudgy windows, some 31 odd pairs of eyes in each classroom watched us pass. Some waved or winked. I winced, knowing how little the teachers would appreciate the late-afternoon distraction.

Finally Mr. Hollinger took us to an odd building off to the side of the schoolyard that was to become *my* classroom. It was packed with balls and bats and bases, and other rummage from the not-too-active phys. ed. department.

Womanlike, I began calculating what I'd do to make this little shop truly my classroom. Let's see, I could decorate those bulletin boards, and we could make some curtains one day as a class, and I'd shove all the refuse back into neat stacks near the back. It needed sweeping and scrubbing, but it would be *my* home base! Here I would teach the girls about sewing and cooking; we'd talk about boys and parents; and finally, I hoped to discover whether I'd really like to be a teacher the rest of my life.

Mr. Hollinger was proudly describing, "We don't have any sewing machines for you yet, but we're getting three that were donated from a store in town. One's a $200 machine." He paused for effect. "The other two are used."

"Oh, that will be fine," I assured him. Let's see, I figured, if I have 15 girls, that will be only five to a machine. Still too many. I'd have to divide the girls and have them come in for only one period a week, so that each could work with her own machine.

"And the cooking classes, where will I do those?" I asked the principal. I don't know if I'd expected to see a fully equipped, modern, home economics lab with all the luxuries like I'd had in junior high, but there weren't even any stoves or sinks in *this* hole.

"You can use the cafeteria—the school kitchen," he replied matter-of-factly.

"But the cooks, won't they have to be using it?" I asked.

22

"Oh, they go home about 1:30 each day. You can use the kitchen after that." At least he had everything thought out.

It would hardly be the neat, orderly arrangement I'd hoped for, but it would be better than nothing.

"As soon as you're ready to start classes, the girls will be ready for you," Mr. Hollinger was saying. "They're really looking forward to it."

"Well, it will take a couple of weeks to get organized, and we shouldn't even have to wait for the sewing machines," I explained. "We'll start with a cooking unit. I'll let you know when we can schedule the first class."

We shook hands all around.

School was out, and some of the children were standing in the schoolyard waiting for the bus to come back and pick up a second load of kids. Someone had already found out my name and yelled, "Hi, Melodie!" How had the news traveled so fast? It was my first introduction to the efficiency of the news network in a small place like Troublesome Creek. I smiled bravely in the direction of the call, wondering which of these children would be my friends, and which would be more interested in making life painful for the teacher.

One little boy especially captured me. His eyes were dull, not from inborn mental weakness, but from breakfasting on soda pop and Twinkies, from suppers of mashed potatoes and greasy gravy. His clothes were smudged with a week's worth of playground grime and nose dirt. His hair must have been chopped off by a sister. But most striking of all, he stood apart—just watching the others play, like an untouchable.

Could I possibly make a difference in that little life? Probably not, but I was both glad and scared to be here, to have the responsibility to *try*.

# 3

# Whew! It's nice to have the honeymoon over!

In many ways, I felt like the legendary stranger in a strange land. Odd-sounding English bombarded my ears as I listened to the kindergarten children chatter on the way to school in the unit van:

poke     (sack or bag)
narry    (hardly)
h'its    (it is)
h'ain't    (it ain't)
rait chere    (right here)
least 'un    (youngest)
tared    (tired)
flare    (flower)

The fair skin topped by rosy cheeks (at least on the healthier ones) made the children look like they'd walked straight out of the pages of a *National Geographic* article on Scotland.

The foods they talked about were just as foreign: shucky beans, stack cake, pollet sallet, collard greens.

And so the first week of voluntary service flew by in a kind of traveler's cultural shock: I rushed to take pictures, recorded impressions in my journal, and in general soaked up my new atmosphere like a sapling freshly transplanted.

I gaped at the tumbledown houses and pitied the diaperless children clamoring over frazzled-looking mothers on front porches. I wondered at the ballet-like grace which carried the kindergartners nonchalantly across treacherous swinging bridges lacing Troublesome Creek. I kept remembering the cruel epithet—"hillbilly"—we had tossed around in my childhood to refer to these proud, hard-working mountain people who had migrated to our area to seek good paying work. As I stared and photographed, already the stereotypes began to topple as I met little beauties called Michael, Stevie, Jackie, Tammy, Michelle, Ricky, Dora, and more.

The kindergarten was Judi's domain. At that time the public schools did not provide kindergarten, and many of the children needed this extra advantage much more than their counterparts in neighboring, richer states.

So an important function of the VS unit was the kindergarten, operated cooperatively through the local Mennonite church. Students were charged a nominal fee, if they could pay. The money was used to help purchase snacks and supplies. The fact that there was a charge helped parents take more responsibility in sending their children regularly. For an hour each morning, the unit van navigated the steep and crooked (and often muddy) mountain roads to ferry the children to kindergarten.

The first morning that I rode along the route, I jiggled, leaned, bounced, and braced myself—and even caught my breath a time or two. Soon I learned to let my body hang loose like the children did—so that the impact of the turns and jolts didn't cause my whole body to ache. It was an art to let your head sit loose on your shoulders, like a marionette. But it was the only way to survive the daily two hours of "holler" driving without a headache.

I was asked to observe Judi in the kindergarten class for one week—what a crash course in early childhood education! Judi had a degree in it, though, and a way with children that soon made me eager to start my nursery class.

Afternoons I pored over her education books and curriculum materials, collecting ideas for finger plays, exercises, songs, crafts, nursery rhymes, pictures to color, and bulletin board displays. Somehow it seemed like I was only preparing for a two-week stint of summer Bible school. I had to keep pinching myself that I—the ink barely dry on my high school diploma—was going to have these students for eight whole months! Was it fair to the children to send one so lightly prepared to be their teacher? If enthusiasm and love for little ones were all that it took, I knew I would do fine. I kept focusing on my goal: to help the children get a head start in school so they could feel good about themselves and be successes in school, life, and forever after!

But all those carefully written objectives drooped as I faced my little charges that first day. There was Vonda, who had a penchant for smearing crumbs from ear to ear during snack time; Stevie, who cried for his mother all morning; Kasandra, who insisted that her mother wanted her to be dropped off at Rachel's store rather than at her doorstep (we knew better); Vicki, a delightfully pretty little girl, who seemed to have little need of nursery school; and Donald Gene, who refused to talk, even to grunt, nod, smile, or otherwise communicate. They colored out of lines, and some had never seen a scissors. They didn't know how to stand in a circle or line. Somehow, we all got through that first morning, and Judi said it would probably be my hardest day.

I called home that evening, and had my first rush of homesickness. The thought of being away for a whole year, living in an apartment with friendly strangers who seemed to watch TV a lot, all seemed a bit much. Why had I been so eager to push out of the nest? Like the too-brave baby bird, I was floundering in a job for which I had virtually no preparation, no past experience. What I didn't know was that practically all first-days-on-the-job go like that. The high hopes for being a brilliant whatever suddenly come crashing to reality in the confusion of new faces, names, routines, how-to's and one's own human limitations.

I reflected on how the two weeks of preparation at VS headquarters had done little to prepare me for facing my own inadequacies. Orientation had been an intense immersion in people, group discussion, films, counseling, recreation, worship, and eating. It was heady—like having a mountaintop retreat-type experience last two whole weeks— little concern for time, weather, the news, TV—the ordinary stuff that makes up most people's days. It was like life had been suspended, and now was resuming a routine—going to work, lunch, working some more, supper, and amusing oneself until bedtime. At orientation, the main pastime was getting to know the other persons. Here there were other concerns. And I had to remember that they all knew each other already—I was the intruder.

After I finished my call home, I stayed up with the other VSers to watch a detective thriller on TV. A good feeling of togetherness came over me, like we had all been stranded in a blizzard at the same interstate restaurant. We all experienced the same fear, anxiety, and suspense—uniting us, paradoxically, with barely uttering a word. I hoped that there would be nights of good discussion, recreation, and fellowship, too, but somehow it was nice to know that VS units sometimes relaxed in front of the TV. It was comforting to know that VSers weren't always out nobly leading boys' clubs and conducting prayer meetings.

But I was glad the next day when Judi and Lawrence suggested we spend the afternoon visiting Ernest, a blind man who lived in a nearby holler. Aha! Now *this* was one of the things a VS unit was *supposed* to do, I told myself. Visit community persons. This would look good on the monthly activity report sent to headquarters.

In visiting Ernest's humble mountain home, I soon learned he was one of those people who made you feel like he had given more to you than you to him. His garden was remarkable: straight rows of lush, weed-free vegetables for him and his sister to use, to give away, and to sell. Swapping summertime vegetables, as well as advice on gardening signs, was a favorite pastime.

Ernest could tell tales without boring you, and he could listen too—always with a half smile on his face. Leaning on his cane, he was more than just a caricature of a mountain man. His blind eyes were still a breathtaking blue, reminiscent of his proud English ancestry. I often wondered about the accident that claimed his sight, but never had the nerve to ask. His full, worn face, drawn with pleasant laugh and cry lines, was a human portrait of kindness and honesty, with the forthrightness that makes a plain person beautiful.

Ernest kept himself in shape and in touch by daily walking the 1½ miles to the store and post office. His cane was his guide to keep him from the plunging mountainsides. Even when the road was slippery and snow-packed, Ernest came to the store and everyone worried about him getting back up the trail safely.

That afternoon I came away feeling at last that I had

really gotten to meet and know one of the local people. I suspected that Judi and Lawrence didn't visit Ernest for *his* sake—to do the noble "VS" thing—but because Ernest and his life spoke to *them*. Here was a man at peace with his world and God, in touch with who he was and his life. I asked myself, "How can he be so together?" In a life defined by the parameters of blindness, he seemed neither discontent nor discouraged with the futility of life. I wanted to take lessons from this man, so that I, still young and limitless in horizons, could receive sight in blind places.

Before supper, Judi sent me down to the store for some bread all by myself and I felt like an old hand giving Bert a warm "Howdy," telling him to "charge it," and taking the whistles in stride without a glimmer of embarrassment (I hoped). On the way out of the store, I stopped to chat with a young girl waiting beside the edge of the road. She was about my age, so I told her who I was and that I was new to the unit. In that brief pause, I must have grown up at least ten years. She was worrying about where she could get enough money for a divorce.

Suddenly my accent and nicer clothes were the least of things that separated us: we were culturally, socially, and every other way as far distant as I was from home. Dumbly, I shuffled back upstairs to the unit apartment.

My task had taken on a new dimension. Would little Vonda or Vicky grow up to be in that young girl's situation? What did teaching finger plays like "Eensy beensie spider" have to do with love and marriage and divorce? How could I in four short hours a week, eight short months of a lifetime, do anything to start a direction?

I knew I couldn't, and I prayed.

# 4

# Everything you always wanted to know about what goes on in a houseful of unrelated people

G'mornin." I stumbled past Dave in the hall on my way to the apartment's only bathroom. Dave was a medical technologist at the local hospital, and usually got up long before I did. But this weekend he had a four-day stretch off. He looked puffy-eyed, unshaven, and terribly undressed in his white T-shirt and pair of old pants. I clutched my bathrobe tighter and wished the curlers off my head. It felt strange to be in my bathrobe within several feet of a man who wasn't even my brother. Although the stories of VS romances and marriages are popular, my unscientific research has it that more persons *don't* get romantically involved than do. In one quick encounter, I just learned why.

Breakfasts on Saturday mornings were a lazy, long meal of eggs, pancakes, orange juice, and coffee.

"How'd you sleep?" asked Judi.

"Um—good. Until the coal trucks and the banging of the store door woke me up." I sighed my familiar lament.

"Better ask Rachel how *she* slept," teased Marlin, with a smile in his eyes. Marlin had an open-ended community service assignment, primarily teaching woodworking to junior high boys. Rachel was an R.N. and the kind of person who could walk up to a strange lady and tell her that her slip was showing. I felt at home with her immediately. So she made no secret of the fact that I was a mean kicker in my sleep. Sound sleeper that I was, I had no memory of my mulish tendencies or of her futile efforts to nudge me back to my side of the bed.

"I was tempted to get up and go around to get in on the other side," Rachel said, but she smiled good-naturedly.

But I knew she couldn't go on losing sleep like that, especially when she had to get up so early for her 7:00 a.m. shift at the hospital.

"I really am embarrassed," I said, making a face. "I was used to sleeping by myself, since my sister left for college two years ago." I felt terrible. I knew there was no room in the unit budget for single beds—let alone space in our small room. What would VS headquarters think of me, causing so many problems already?

Marlin's eyes were still playful. "I think we've got an answer for you two." We all looked at him. "Lawrence says we can squeeze some cash out of the budget for some lumber, and it shouldn't be too difficult for me to build a set of bunk beds."

I could have kissed him. The perfect solution. No wonder he had brought up a "sore" point.

"VSers really shouldn't have to sleep in double beds anyway," said Lawrence. "This place has been needing single beds for a long time."

"So headquarters won't be mad at me?" I asked, half-seriously.

"They'll just be glad we've finally got our accommodations up to par," Lawrence reassured me.

One of my first shocks was finding out that a VS unit was made up of persons mostly like myself. I had the notion that the girls would fix their hair in buns and not wear slacks—that the guys would sport white socks and crew cuts. I thought there'd be devotions morning, noon, and night with everyone praying in King James English.

I was also worried that I'd get into a "bad" unit. I'd heard horror stories of units where there were splits, divorces, slave drivers, boozers, and hellfire preachers. Instead of such intense conflicts and involvement, our unit seemed very opposite—loose and uncommitted. Although there were warm moments, like when Marlin announced the good news about making bunk beds for us. But on the whole relationships were so good they seemed superficial, conversations so light it didn't seem like people cared about each other. And while I was relieved that they weren't a bunch of goody-goodies, I was not accustomed to this type of spiritual commitment. To me the most unifying weekly experience was watching a detective show on TV!

I was intrigued, though, about the communal aspects of living in a VS unit. Essentially Dave and Rachel were the breadwinners, while the rest of us were "community workers." Their incomes, which were channeled into the VS headquarters overall budget, allowed us the freedom of working at jobs without pay. In turn, we cooked their meals and tried to be family. Communes were the lifestyle that many of us gossiped about in those days, so it felt just a little bit daring to be living in a type of commune right within the framework of the Mennonite Church. Oh, it wasn't the kind of commune that had loose attitudes towards everything from clothes to morals, but one where cooperative approaches to labor still made for some raised eyebrows in the community.

One day Marlin hung around the kitchen after lunch, dried the dishes, put them away, and wiped the table and counters. Finally when we were through sweeping the floor, I found out his motive.

"Uh, Mel, I was wondering if you'd mind ironing my shirt and slacks for the concert tonight."

"Sure," I said. "Hey, this is just like home where my brother used to butter me up to ask a favor," I thought. But it was a good feeling, to realize this guy I had known for only three weeks was fast becoming like a brother to me.

It was 1970 and pre-women's movement, at least in church circles. So our household unit chores were pretty much divided along traditional lines. The guys mowed, kept the cars serviced, worked in the garden, and pitched in when major chores needed to be done. But the cooking, dishwashing, weekly cleaning, shopping, and laundry fell mostly to the "girls."

To be fair, it was also divided this way by assignment: because neither I nor Judi truly had full workloads with our part-time teaching assignments, the bulk of the housework was ours. As unit hostess, Judi was in charge of meals and cleaning and called on me for assistance. Rachel, who worked a full 40-hour week at the hospital, was *not* expected to pitch in at chore time.

Unit life was not all work. The monthly budget allowed for one paid excursion per month as a unit—to a movie or a concert or eating out. One of our first activities after I joined the unit was attending a local homecoming football game—which was not only entertainment but fit the requirement to "relate to the community." And so having an open-ended "community service" assignment was sometimes a blessing: it allowed you to do community service while enjoying a football game!

As we rushed through supper, dishes, and dressing, with six nonrelated adults trying to use the bathroom at appropriate intervals, somehow the women of the unit were the last ones to scuttle out the door. As we piled into the unit car, the three guys were already in place. I was sure they were furious.

"Well, I might as well say it for everyone," said Lawrence.

I thought, "Oh, no, here it comes. He's going to scold us for taking so long."

Instead, all he said was, "You women look nice. *Very* nice."

I'm not so sure that was the *only* thing on his mind, but at least it was the tactful thing to say. He went up at least two notches in my respect!

One way to achieve quick submersion into local culture is to attend a small-town football game. But by far the most interesting game is played out in the stands—young girls walking by self-consciously sucking their stomachs in, loose huddles of adolescent guys hacking on cigarettes, proud mothers and fathers trying to pick out number 35 on the field, couples who are too young for "car" dates engaged in mutual admiration societies, some unsmiling cops with beer guts menacingly pacing the sidelines. I have absolutely no idea what went on at that game or if "our" side even won.

I had to wonder what the townspeople thought of our odd group as they, too, engaged in people-gazing. Judi and Lawrence—well, they were kosher. They had wedding rings on. But what of the blond, strong-looking woman of about

34

24 (Rachel). Was she with the fellow who looked older too (Dave)? And the girl that looked like she was just out of high school (me). Was she with the younger guy (Marlin)? If so, why didn't they sit or act like couples? And if they were just friends, why did they bother to come together at all?

In a mountain community where marriage at age 14 or 15 is common, and "have to" marriages at that age were even more common, I can imagine that it was almost impossible to believe that unrelated guys and girls could possibly live in the same house without some extracurricular sex going on. Over the years, however, the people who bothered really to get to know the various unit members had come to respect and trust these outsiders with their slightly offbeat lifestyle.

The football field was right next to the hospital where Dave and Rachel worked. One day soon after the homecoming game when Dave was off and Rachel was driving to work alone, she lost control of the car on a wet, treacherous curve. She called home shaken and bruised, but basically unhurt. The guys went after her with another vehicle, and for the rest of the morning we listened, we nursed, we brought cups of hot tea.

That afternoon everyone except Rachel worked at packaging a half a beef. "We used to draw pictures of hands on the packages of hamburger *patties*," I said and I laughed. As the unit taped, wrapped, and marked the beef, the stories flew as fast as our hands. It felt good teaming together like that—almost like an assembly line.

That night—I don't know if it was because of Rachel's accident or packaging the beef—four of us kind of naturally congregated around the piano. We sang hymn after hymn—exactly like I had envisioned VS units doing. The alto wasn't perfect—it was the first time I ever had to carry my part alone.

When we tired, I said, "That reminded me of VS orientation."

"We really should do things like this more often," someone countered, "but VS isn't orientation. Here we're also living—tired, busy, with moods. . . ."

"Yeah, I guess maybe I was hoping we'd have devotions and singing together every night," I ventured.

Lawrence joined in. "I guess some units do. But our approach as unit leaders is to expect it to be more of a personal thing—that we expect that of each other as mature Christians."

I was thinking that I didn't feel so mature, but it suddenly sunk in that I was a good three years younger than the rest. Most of them had been through college—which made me feel even younger. I did have an active personal devotional life, writing in my journal, reading, taking long walks alone.

We prayed together that night—for Rachel, for our work, the church, our families, for community persons we knew. Suddenly I realized that here were people who did know a great deal about each other—after all, they had been together almost a year already and here I was expecting to know intimate truths after roughly three weeks. Here were Christians who were struggling with some of the same things I was—how to know God and his will better, how to relate to the hurting ones in the community, how to *live* their faith. I sensed that, as usual, God knew what he was doing in working it out that I was to live with this particular bunch of his people for a year of my life.

Now the everyday conversation that formerly seemed trite was homey: the kind of stuff you can say only in families and know there's caring behind the clichés. The lack of involvement with each other was respect for each other's space, privacy, and lifestyles. The low level of God-language was in a way reverence—not cheapening it through overuse. Service, love, and trust were important—and at base, a personal relationship to Christ.

I shouldn't have been surprised to find out that people who would enter a program like "Voluntary Service" would have a keen and primary interest in fleshing out a servant lifestyle.

I began to reflect more and more on the nature of service. One night as I was washing dishes I realized that this too was service. Only who was I doing it for and why? For the other unit members? It's probably the lowliest of all tasks, except for scrubbing the toilet. Did my Christian commitment and ideas about servanthood have anything to do with my attitude about serving the other members of the unit in this way? Would it have anything to say ten years down the road as I seethed in dish suds while my husband lounged in the living room after work?

I'd like to be able to say that VS revolutionized my attitude toward washing dishes. Unfortunately, the job remained as distasteful and as unrelenting as ever. But for one brief moment that night I felt fulfilled in the dishpan. This was service!

# 5

# Maybe I'm not cut out to be a teacher after all

Nursery school and the cooking class every afternoon filled my fall days as I made lesson plans, arranged bulletin board displays, found recipes, and gathered supplies. On days that I had adequately done my homework, classes went well and I felt good about my role and the students. On days that I procrastinated, saying, "Well, I'll just kind of play it by ear today," I usually felt frustrated and inadequate. I began to understand that although it seemed like teachers had the easy job in high school, always sending us home with stacks of homework, I knew now that they didn't quit at 3:00 p.m. At least the good ones didn't.

The best part of teaching for me was simply watching and playing with the children, or talking with the junior high girls after school. It wasn't long before I realized that my being available—really present, listening and caring—was probably the hidden reason for sending such an untrained person to a community such as this. It wasn't so much what I had to offer in terms of early childhood education or home economics, but the fact that I had been brought up in a home where *I* was loved, valued, listened to, and I could share *that* training.

I certainly didn't always succeed at that though either. Like the morning Davey was playing with a doll all alone at nursery school, trying to put its pants on. I was intrigued that he often played with dolls. I figured that at home, in this traditional community, he never was allowed to.

I stole a picture with the camera that I took occasionally to nursery school. His look of shock and betrayal made me wish immediately that I had first asked his permission;

"It's okay," I said too quickly. "I just want to get pictures of you children playing at different times," I tried to cover up. But his embarrassed retreat from the dolls told me I had invaded his privacy. Teacher had some learning to do, too.

My students were certainly coming along. Within a few weeks of my first class, I had convinced Vonda it wasn't grown up to smear cookie crumbs all over, Kasandra really tried to color inside the lines, Donald Gene actually smiled and said, "Yes," when I asked him if he had to go to the bathroom, and Stevie asked to go "poddy" instead of using his usual four-letter word. Somehow these small milestones meant more to me than all the "A's" I ever earned in high school. Perhaps as with giving and receiving, it's more blessed to teach than to be taught.

But my impatience with the stronger-willed, stubborn ones disturbed me. It sickened me to have to punish a child, even though it was nothing more than a stern warning and removal to a quiet place to think. Most of these children had had too many slaps and "whoppins" for me to want to add to that tally. Discipline is not my forte. Imitating Judi I tried to be firm though loving, respected yet liked.

One day the little girls were rocking and feeding their doll babies as usual. And the boys started using pretend machine guns to shoot up the babies in a horrible mock version of some war they'd seen on TV. The girls appealed to me, "Make them stop! Make them stop blowing our babies to bits." So I told the girls that it was just pretend, that the boys didn't really mean it. "See your dollies haven't been blown to bits, have they?" The girls believed me, glad it was only "pretend." Of course, I tried to help the boys think of a better game than acting out old war movies.

Switching from four-year-olds to twelve-to-fourteen-year-olds for afternoon sewing class was refreshing. With the junior high girls, I could talk about more weighty topics than dolls and potty use—although I wonder in retrospect whether making pin cushions, aprons, and floppy beach hats was much more relevant to their lives.

One girl who frequently stayed to talk after class was Caroline. She often invited me to come and visit her, so one afternoon Judi and I did just that. She and her family lived at the farthest end of one hollow. "Wolf Pen," it was called. High in the hills, it was accessible only by a red dirt road given to washouts and foot-deep potholes.

When we first pulled up outside her house, my mind said, "Memorize it," thinking of the incident of Davey and the camera. It was a pileup of lean-tos and porches, looking like a new partition had been added everytime a child joined the family. The children emerged curiously from their play and work places at the sound of our approaching vehicle—heard, I imagine, for a long way in the quiet stillness of a Kentucky holler. There were pots of flowers on the porches, washtubs, a wringer washer, strings of dried "shucky beans" hanging from the walls, dried gourds, and ladderback chairs.

Caroline lumbered out of the house with a wide plain grin

on her face. She was larger and older than the other girls from class, as she had fallen behind a year or two in her studies. "Howdy, Melanie . . . Judi." For some reason it was hard for her to remember that my name was Melodie.

"Come in. My momma's inside and she wants to meet ya." I wondered how much she really wanted to meet us, remembering how my own mother scurried about in a futile effort to "pretty the place up" if someone from a better home than ours came to visit.

Inside, the house was dark from pulled shades and plastic curtains. There were pictures of Jesus in Gethsemane and youngish army recruits hung high on the wall. There was a cookstove, a woodstove heater, and clean-scrubbed linoleum throughout.

As we entered the best room of the house, I only gradually became aware that there was a boy in this room who had not ventured out of the house to greet us. He looked eight or ten in age, but lounged like an eight-month-old—unable to walk, crawl, or even support himself. Caroline had never mentioned a brother like this at home. But from my first moments in that living room, it was obvious that the whole family doted on him like a baby—amused him, carried him from room to room, talked baby talk to this child-boy, and never mentioned him outside the home. Likely he was seldom taken to any public place—loved and protected by his family—his lot in life as accepted as mining accidents and illegitimate babies. Time after time in our visits to homes we learned of these hidden family members—and that part of the reason for so many mentally retarded persons was the inbreeding and marriages between too close of relatives, and the fact that many women had babies almost every year—sometimes well into their forties.

Caroline was proudly pointing out the stereo that her

41

sister, in her late twenties, had been able to buy for the family. "Yeah, buddy, Sis has a good job in town." I wondered what pitiful sum she was paid, or where she worked. From her picture I could tell she was attractive, and I wondered why she had not yet married, why she still lived at home providing for this family.

"If you stay jes' a little longer, she'll be home and'll fix ya some supper," Caroline pleaded. She looked so genuine that there was no way to doubt the sincerity of her invitation.

"Caroline, I'll come back sometime and have supper with you," I promised, and knew I would have to keep my word. I wondered how I would force myself to drink from the water bucket and dipper that sat on the long, oilclothed kitchen table.

Caroline was radiant. She talked us all the way to our Scout, and stood waving till we rounded the first bend. What kind of future would she have, I wondered. I chuckled to myself at the thought of *me* trying to teach this daughter from such a self-sufficient family anything about cooking or sewing. I didn't even know how to fire up a cookstove.

That evening at supper Marlin mentioned that he heard that Judi and I had driven all the way up Wolf Pen Holler to the Williamses.

"You were in Hazard all day. How on earth . . . ." I tried to figure out how the news had traveled so fast.

"Well, I was in the store this evening and the fellas were talking about seeing you two women bouncing up the holler in the Scout. One of 'em was Donnie." Marlin's eyes wore that playful glint again.

"Who's Donnie?" I wanted to know.

"Just one of the nicest fellows in this community," Lawrence chimed in.

I tried to be casual. "He's not the one who drives the blue

pickup that's often parked in front of the store in the morning and evening?"

"Yeah, that's the one."

"Seriously, Melodie, he really is a nice guy."

"He lives with his mom and dad, who are in failing health," Judi added. "Works out at one of the strip mines running big equipment."

"Oh, a strip miner," I said, dismayed. Anyone who could help tear away these beautiful mountains didn't especially interest me.

After supper I climbed into my favorite perch on the front porch, to write in my journal. It was a perfect hideaway from which to watch the goings and comings of the whole community, and for the most part hidden from the view of the teenagers who lounged about the store front. I looked across to the house that Marlin had said this Donnie fellow lived in. His blue truck was home. I wondered again how anyone with any feeling for the good earth could be any part of such a brutal destruction. It would be nice to get to know a fellow in this community. But as I surveyed the ones slouching by the light pole in the growing darkness, their loud laughter told me that they were getting drunk again. They threw beer cans down the hill to our garden, now empty for the fall. If I had entered VS to meet a guy, the Lord was certainly teaching me a lesson for having such shallow motives. These didn't even measure up to the guy I hadn't wanted to marry at home. Or was I being too picky, too narrow-minded, too prejudiced?

Just as I was getting ready to leave my nook, one of the guys—a redhead, spied me. He was cute I thought, and at least not so obviously 14 or 15—probably a bare 17. "Hey, beautiful," he called as I wanted to melt to a grease spot. I had seen him around and knew only the alcohol had given

43

him enough courage to call out to this foreigner "schoolteacher." I slid into the house, chilled, embarrassed, and lonely.

What was I doing in this isolated little village anyway, I thought angrily. Why did these people hide away their retarded, tear up some of their land, and litter the rest, seemingly accepting their lot in life with no desire to better themselves. (Or was I just trying to impose my value system?) Wasn't I just a glorified babysitter at nursery school—freeing moms for three short morning hours to take care of their babies? What would ever happen to Caroline? She'd probably marry a second or third cousin at 16 and end up with a boy to hide of her own. And whip up greasy suppers on a cookstove—the finer skills of baking party tea cakes and blueberry muffins long since rendered useless.

Suddenly next September seemed a lifetime away. How could I bear not to see my parents for a whole year? It was nice when Judi's and Lawrence's parents had come to visit from Maryland and Pennsylvania. I even felt like they were my surrogate parents, playing Scrabble on Sunday afternoons and eating popcorn. I knew my own parents, as farmers, were too hard up at the moment to come visit me. Although a VSer was allowed a week of vacation time in a year of service, it wasn't considered proper to take that vacation within the first four months.

I wondered what headquarters would think if I went home for Christmas. It would probably just reinforce the notion that 18-year-olds are a little immature to handle a whole year away from home. Worse, how could I afford it? I had a small cash hoard saved from my summer waitressing job.

It was probably a wild shot, but I decided to check into bus fares and schedules the next day. If I could just make it to December and go home for Christmas, maybe I could get through the whole year.

# 6

## People impressions

I don't know when Rachel, for whom the store at Ary was named, first introduced me to her colorful collection of patchwork art. At first glance they might have seemed just ordinary quilt or "comfort" (Southern lingo) tops. But when you learned that Rachel had cut and pieced each tiny square by hand—all at 80 plus years, these homespun creations became her lifework, her discipline, every bit as much a work of art as something on exhibit in New York City.

Rachel was a humpbacked small-framed woman who became tinier each passing year as time drew her body together. But the cheerful, warm eyes betrayed an inner spirit that did not draw into itself. She was vitally interested in the VSers who came into her life and then out again.

On my very first visit to her home, she asked, half modestly, but with a hint of pride that persons over 80 wear well, "Do you want to see my quilt tops?" She pulled open a bureau drawer and lifted out a crazy bright top.

"Oh, Rachel," I gasped. "Isn't that pretty! Did you really piece it all by hand?"

In answer she pulled out another top.

"This 'uns a flower garden quilt, and it's a-goin' to my great niece."

"That's beautiful," I said, and meant it. We pulled out top after top, unfolded and folded them back up. Sometimes she'd point to a person in one of the many family pictures jamming her bureau top as the recipient of a particular quilt.

Finally, Goldie, her daughter, came in and suggested that maybe I'd seen enough now, that maybe I was busy. And Rachel scurried back to her patchwork. I learned to go to Rachel's when I was feeling homesick, depressed, or lonely.

Like the time early in November when Judi and Lawrence took vacation and I was left in charge of the meals for a whole week. One of the unit members families' also chose that weekend to come and visit, so I had my chance to prepare my very first Sunday dinner, without any supervision from mom. The roast wasn't done, the potatoes became discolored during cooking, the carrots were hard, the cabbage was mushy, the salad too tangy, there were no dinner rolls in the house, and I forgot all about making dessert until it was too late.

One of the family members, Marg, came to my room after dinner. "Please don't worry about the dinner, Mel. It wasn't that bad. Just think, every cook is entitled to at least one meal disaster. Now you won't have to worry about creating that first flop for your husband—you've got it over with!"

Marg looked so cheerful, so convincing, that I believed her, especially since she didn't try to tell me it was delicious. Marg was the kind of person who made me feel inferior without even trying. She bubbled charm, enthusiasm, energy, wittiness. Tall and blond with blue eyes, she was not

46

only pretty, but also had the nerve to be so nice one couldn't help liking her.

Why did I have to be so reserved, so solemn? Why didn't people huddle around me admiring every word the way they do around the Margs of this world, I wondered. Sometimes it's hard to believe that God even likes those of us who are not quite so outgoing.

After Marg left my room, I somehow felt better, in spite of feeling inadequate. Maybe it was remembering one of the things I had learned in VS orientation—that God didn't ask us to be resounding successes in what we did, that all he asked us to be was *faithful*. And so if I felt inadequate, I could try to improve my personality—not to be a carbon copy of someone else, but to become the person I really wanted to be.

After a week of trying to cook perfectly balanced meals to please four different palates at $1.00 per person per day and get it all on the table at the same time with hot foods piping and cold foods chilled—I jumped at the chance to get away for the weekend.

My roommate, Rachel, invited me to go with her to a friend's parents' home in western Kentucky. After seven weeks of isolation in eastern Kentucky, the shopping center alone in that mid-sized town was enough to send me into culture-shock. Everything reminded me of my growing up days in Indiana: neat countryside farms and homes, the whiff of toasting leaves, slightly crisp "basketball season" air, eating at a Big Boy hamburger joint.

On Saturday afternoon we accompanied Rachel's friend to the laundromat. Two young wives in curlers were there, preparing for a night out, gossiping about who was running around on whom. They were struggling with three preschoolers between them, about the soda pop they couldn't have and the candy bars they shouldn't smear on each other.

Suddenly I felt so smug not to be tied to a laundromat and 2.2 screaming kids on a lovely November afternoon, glad that a wise camp counselor had once advised me: "Melodie, have you ever considered what you'll do with your life if you *don't* get married in a year or two?" Marriage and kids would be all right someday, but maybe I could give more to a husband and kids if I wasn't in too big a hurry.

The host where we stayed for the weekend was full of stories—about the "nigger" shanties that still lined neighboring farms, about the "good uns" and "bad uns" he had known. As always such talk stung my ears, sensitive because of long years of being taught that "we're all the same in God's sight" and because of the many black friends and visitors that had come through my childhood home. But as I listened to this 75-year-old man, whose attitudes and perspective were even more ingrained than mine, for once I could listen without becoming deaf by outrage. Was it wrong to accept this bigoted man, without condoning the bigotry? Wasn't it just as wrong for me to be bigoted about a bigot?

Although racial change has come slowly, too slowly, I had to think of the Kentucky of 75 years ago, barely five years removed from slavery. Here was a man who'd seen much change in his lifetime. And while some older folks seem to mellow with change, even those that don't still have worth, and are persons loved by God.

The weekend in western Kentucky was the lull before the beginning of Christmas busyness—a tea party to plan for the junior high girls, a program at church, a party for the nursery schoolers, a time for the unit to celebrate together. It looked like it would barely all fit in, let alone my secret plans to escape home for Christmas. Trying to remember the punch bowl, wrapping gifts for my little nursery schoolers, choosing appropriate gifts for unit members on a VS allowance, I was overflowing with ideas and activities.

Adding to the tumult was the addition of a new VSer, Louise, who was also a registered nurse. She would replace Rachel, but their terms overlapped about a month. So we bunked three girls and junk in a room too small for two.

In the rush, mostly I forgot about my inner restlessness, the feeling that I wasn't getting much accomplished, and that although I knew plenty of people here, I was close to no one. Sure, there were isolated moments of feeling close, like a drive home from a regional 4-H potluck supper when I learned about some of the frustrations of another VSer. It was a new feeling for me—to drive 40 some miles with a young "eligible" male and relate to him as a person, not a "date." In a society that mostly insists that male-female relationships are either romantic or between relatives, it's rare to feel close to a member of the opposite sex without having that relationship romanticized. Oh, with uneligible men it's okay—engaged, married, too old, or too young—these we can be friends with. But an unattached unrelated male of near the same age? Marriage is the automatic, assumed goal.

One day in the madness before Christmas, I was lucky enough to have the unit apartment to myself for several hours one afternoon. That was one thing I definitely missed in voluntary service—the privacy to be truly by myself for hours at a stretch. So I put one of my favorite albums on the stereo, and settled into an overstuffed chair just to knit and think. Glen Campbell was singing about the "man who goes through life, comes here against his will, and goes away disappointed." As the record ended, the silence blanketed the room.

Somehow that song had never hit me before in such a low moment. Was that indeed all there was to life—a series of disappointments? I went to the piano seeking an answer—an answer that because of my upbringing I already knew—but that needed a fresh response for that day. I found just the song—not only because it spoke to my need of the moment, but because it didn't have any sharps or flats and was simple enough for me to play!

### Teach Me Thy Truth*

Teach me thy truth, O mighty one;
From sin O make me free;
Prepare my life to fill its place
In service, Lord, for thee.

Accept my talents, great or small,
Choose thou the path for me,
Where I shall labor joyously
In service, Lord, for thee.

Help me to show thy glorious way
That leads in hope to thee,
Till other souls their joy shall find,
In service, Lord, for thee.

Grant me thy grace for every task
Until thy face I see,
Then ever new shall be that joy
In service, Lord, for thee.
      Amen.

---

*Hymn words by Edith Witmer, copyright by Mennonite Publishing House.

# 7

# Homesick

Travel arrangements were finally made. I knew that the 24-hour bus trip by way of Lexington, Louisville, Birmingham, and Montgomery would be rough. But I was in no way prepared for the layover in Birmingham from 2:30 to 6:30 a.m. The night people wandered in and out of the station, catching a few winks in the partitioned benches and rummaging through wastebaskets. With my bright red suitcases, I stuck out like Rudolph's nose—wealthy (at least in comparison), female, and very much alone. I prayed and wondered what mom would think if she could see where her youngest daughter was.

At 5:00 a.m. the cafeteria opened up and at least I could find solace in an unspoken companionship with the cafeteria attendant. I ordered a big breakfast of spicy sausages, eggs, juice, and coffee, and lingered over every bite as though I was eating at the Waldorf Astoria.

When I finally arrived home, I was surprised how big my

room looked, how much taller my brother was, and that I had forgotten where things went in mom's kitchen. Although it was incredibly good to sack out on my own bed and have mom wake me up in time for supper, for the first time I felt the bittersweetness of knowing it would never truly be home again. You *can't* go home again, not when you have a new room, a new life to compare to the old, new friends and faces greeting you every morning at the breakfast table. The urgency of last September to be "on my own" seemed premature as I began to realize what I had left—forever. Oh, sure, there would be vacations at home. Maybe I would even choose to live at home for a year or more sometime. But it would never be the same, now that I knew how other people lived on day-to-day basis.

Like the toddler or adolescent who grieves yet welcomes a growing separation from mother, I also learned the sweeter side of growing up, entering into those special, wonderful years of relating to mom and dad as adults. Of course, that pass wasn't accomplished in one short trip home, but for the first time I really felt like an equal sitting around the kitchen table with mom and my sister talking until midnight about boys and church and dad and college and VS.

And I felt grown up to thank mom and dad for hosting the entire youth group on Sunday evening for games and messy Cracker Jacks. Over hot chocolate, I had spent a lot of time eyeing the best-looking guy in the youth group.

Sometimes he seemed interested, yet so distant. And since I wasn't one to come right out and flirt, that's where things stayed—distant. In my room that night, sharing a bed again with my sister, I found myself aching—physically aching to be held and loved. Why was I in VS, where my dreams of meeting a husband were now to me laughable? The guys in the unit were like brothers, at church there were no young people my age, and the community guys were a world apart. "Why did you make people to be sexually responsive, when we have to hold off for so long—until a marriage that might never be?" I silently asked the dark ceiling of my bedroom.

I wondered why I couldn't be more like my sister. She had plenty of boyfriends, yet she wasn't especially interested in ever getting married or having a family. The guys tonight, as always, were attracted to her charm and wittiness like cats being teased with strings. But I couldn't help but love her, too. I told myself that I was just an introvert instead of an extrovert. But introvert sounded inferior, not as good.

Funny that I had learned, especially in Kentucky, to be so accepting of "rednecks," "fundamentalists," and perfectionists, but yet I hadn't yet learned to accept or love myself.

"Linda," I finally said, punching my sister. "Are you still awake?"

"Um."

"Tonight was fun, wasn't it?" I went on, wanting somehow to tell her some of what I was feeling.

"Yeah, even though I'm in college, I always enjoy coming back to the kids here," she said.

"Remember long ago when I got so mad at you I shoved a whole case of eggs at you in the packing room?" I ventured.

She giggled in the same way that had so maddened me that day in the chicken house. Only now it was chummy, two sisters laughing off an old argument.

"Sometimes I still get mad at you, jealous of how easily you get along with guys," I said.

"I don't do anything special." I felt her shrug. "You just have to be more relaxed, and not worry so much about it. Just be yourself."

"I know."

We were close, as close as any two people in my family,

and yet there was this nagging jealousy that made me unhappy. Maybe it was long-ago memories of well-meaning aunts and uncles who showered praise on her skills as dad's farm helper or athletic prowess. Whatever it was, I couldn't quite shrug it off like I could my feelings about Marg this past fall, around whom I had felt inferior too. Perhaps living in a VS unit is easier, really, than living in a family. The jealousies and hard feelings that develop in VS occur while you're a relatively mature person, and you can cope as a mature person. Many family jealousies are long-standing and ingrown so that you can hardly understand them yourself.

"Good night," I finally said, but she had already dropped off to sleep.

In the morning I wondered why I felt so terrible the night before. Things always looked different in the morning for me. I knew that although my trip home had been short, I was ready to go back to Kentucky. My suitcase was by my bed, open and neatly packed for the trip. My shoes sat beside it, just waiting to get going. And although I would probably never be just like my sister, there were a bunch of kids in Kentucky who called me teacher, friend, leader.

I thought I went "home" for Christmas. But when I got back to the old apartment over the little store on Troublesome Creek, I knew that was where my heart was then. One of my seventh-graders called and asked if I couldn't "please come and conduct sewing classes today." I said, "No, I just got back but I'll be there tomorrow." It was so good to be missed and wanted.

I was anxious to see my nursery schoolers, too. There's something about four-year-olds—so natural and fresh from the hand of God—that usually makes me smile.

Davey did not disappoint me. I knew again I was in God's place for me when he came on Monday morning and

54

proudly shoved one slightly rotten apple into my hand.

Although it was January, it wasn't particularly cold or snowy. My waistline told tales of the holidays and four months of not wanting to offend a unit hostess. I began to seek fun ways to exercise. One outlet was dribbling around an outdoor basketball court—although I could practically hear the gossip rippling up and down the hollers. Often community guys came up to the unit to borrow the unit's basketball so I had to take advantage of it when it wasn't in use.

The court was in a deserted cove behind the elementary school, sheltered on one side by a steep mountain slope. It was a great place to think, as well as star in imaginary championship games where I was shooting the crucial free throw.

One evening after I had been playing solitaire basketball for 45 minutes or more—the flush of a nippy January day dabbing my cheeks—I noticed a whole gang of guys advancing slowly toward the court. It looked like 12—must have only been a half dozen—but they approached with sneers on their faces of "wonder what she's gonna do?"

For a moment I debated playing with them—I knew several by name—but I also knew that this just wasn't done—one female VSer with a half dozen teenage guys.

"Here," I said too brightly, tossing the ball. "Maybe you can bring the ball back to the unit when you're through." A fellow named James Larry caught the ball and smiled, but no one said anything. I turned and walked quickly to the apartment, resisting the urge to turn and look.

I was half mad—that my exercise time had been stopped short, that I had to worry about what others would think if I played with them, that I hadn't been brave enough to talk to them. What was I scared of—with mostly 17-to-18-year-olds?

Were our cultures so different or was I just plain stuck-up? Did I have some secret need to show off by flaunting rusty high school ball-handling skills?

It was a 14-year-old friend from church who supplied part of my answer.

He was my first and favorite friend from the little mountain church the VS unit attended, an awkward-aged boy with a fluff of blond hair and wide blue eyes.

"Hi, I'm Winky," were his first words to me, said in a disarming, matter-of-fact way that assumed I would like him.

When he said Winky, all *I* could think of was a book I read once that starred a horse named Winky. I said, "Oh, I once knew a horse named "Winky."

And he said, "Well, then you can call me "Horse."

I laughed and "Horse" laughed—even though the name never made sense to anyone else but us.

The first time Judi and I visited him and his elderly grandfather, Elhana, was a Sunday afternoon in fall. Winky stood on the porch smiling a toothy welcome. He knew enough about an "outside" world to know that his home was simple, yet he welcomed us without apology.

We discovered a mutual interest in mountain climbing, and he promised that if I wanted to someday, he'd climb with me to visit an old family burial plot high on the mountains close to his home. Because of our age difference, there was no worry that he'd misread my intentions. So I felt like I was on a walk with my kid brother when I finally took him up on his offer in mid-January. The scenery was desolate, but it turned out to be the best time for such a climb because the underbrush wasn't as hard to get through.

"How do they ever get a hearse and casket up this hill," I wanted to know—for the trail was not one even a jeep could master.

Winky smiled. "It's pretty rough—especially if there's a lot of snow. The pallbearers carry the casket up the mountain."

"Whew," I said appreciatively, being winded without even carrying anything with me. "Well, why did they ever choose such a hard-to-reach place for a cemetery?"

"I think it has something to do with wanting to be closer to heaven—the first to greet Jesus when he comes again," Winky said thoughtfully. "Plus when the creeks rise after spring rains you never have to worry about the cemetery flooding out." He paused. "I don't know. Maybe it was just an old custom."

I was satisfied. All three made sense to me. Winky told me about his brothers and sisters, some of who had migrated to better jobs in Ohio, Michigan, Indiana.

"In the summer when you see Cadillacs and Continentals huggin' the roads, you know people have come in to visit their folks back here in the hollers," Winky continued. "And I mean you better get over on the road. They're not about to."

I smiled, thinking of the all-white town I grew up in and the big cars we had condemned some of the poorer folks for driving. And of the mountain accents I knew they had.

Winky's grandfather, Elhana, had been the first local member of the little church we attended, and Winky was one of the few young men who continued attending church beyond the Sunday school years.

"What do you want to do when you get older?" I asked as we kept climbing.

"I don't know. I wonder about that sometimes, too. Should I go North like my relatives?" Then he grimaced. "I want to finish school." In that part of the country, that in itself would be an accomplishment. He looked embarrassed for not having planned his future better. The fatalism that pervaded these mountains touched everything from little preparation for a career, to accepting the littered roadside as part of life, to a stoic attitude toward death, to the strip mining that ravaged the mountainsides. What would be, would be.

"That's okay," I said finally. "You know, I really don't know what I want to do either. I never have, really."

"Oh, I thought sure you were gonna be a teacher. Your kids—Vonda, Davey—the ones I know—all love you. You're cut out for it."

"Thank you," I said, "but I'm not so sure. I love being *with* the kids, but I don't enjoy disciplining them—having to tell them 'no' constantly, being so strict." He was the first one I had ever dared tell.

"And the kids at the elementary school—they all really look up to you," he added. Then he stopped. "Except I heard one boy say he thought you were stuck-up."

My stomach drew tight. I felt like I had sunk inches into the rock. "Stuck-up." Someone had seen through my facade of shyness, of being quiet, and labeled me for what I really was at times—a conceited, self-centered do-gooder who was too proud to let down my guard for fear of being rejected.

Winky hadn't noticed the hole in my balloon, because he tossed it off as just a lighthearted comment.

Of all the things I didn't want to be to these people, it was that.

We finally reached the dilapidated tombstones. They were edged by a rickety old picket fence all the way around. Quietly we studied the names—Richie, Fugate, Williams. There were some sad, small stones—infant ones, I presumed—with names and dates long washed away by the weather. Some old faded plastic flowers were strewn about, too. We examined an ancient tree, and without saying much, started back down the mountain.

We hiked mostly in silence, and the further we went the more refreshed I felt. Maybe it was the exhilaration of a fresh January day, the pure mountain air, the rare washing that comes when you have risked being truly open with someone. Maybe I had left some of my false pride there on the mountain, in an unlabeled grave. Whatever it was, I felt as though I was walking three feet off the ground, and my body, though sore, was like a steam engine that could roll on for miles.

"We'll have to do that again sometime," Winky and I agreed, when we finally got back to his home.

"I enjoyed it so much," I said. "I love to hike but can't really venture too far on my own for fear of getting lost or running into unfriendly natives."

"Yeah," he agreed, "It's not safe to go too far by yourself."

I drove back to the unit apartment with a new resolve to be more friendly, to really risk reaching out.

# 8

# What happens when a VSer falls in love?

To say "strip-mining" in Kentucky in 1970 was like saying "nuclear arms" in 1980: it was sure to evoke a lively discussion.

Strip-mining in Kentucky in 1970 meant jobs: better jobs because you didn't have to be afraid that your husband wouldn't return from the belly of the earth one day. It meant cheaper coal. It meant "big money" by selling the mineral rights to a mountain on your property that you never expected to get anything out of anyway. Government intervention in strip-mining meant the "government is trying to run our lives" and is "making our coal more expensive by forcing reclamation"—an attempt to restore the land to useful purpose.

Strip-mining in Kentucky in 1970 also meant thousands of acres of raped, ravished, ruined land; streams that were once clear running are red with the soil and minerals and waste from mining areas. It meant unsuspecting landowners ripped off once again by big business and by the wheeling-dealing politicians. It meant "a cause" for students, poets, idealists, and "foreigners"—those who'd left the cities in search of the land.

And, for some native folk, it meant great sadness—sadness to see mountains they'd always loved, that they'd considered "theirs" beyond any title deed—broken. Used. To see trees that had taken 25-to-50 years to mature, suddenly rooted out by an uncaring, upchucking backhoe.

But this fate for their beloved land was accepted like any other of the tragedies that came to their lives. "It's our lot in life," they'd say. "Who are we to fight against God?" (Or the company store?)

Into this land I stumbled like a star-struck child of the 70s. Here was a cause to support! Here was a voice I could raise! Here was a poem to write, a song to compose. I visited an old strip-mining site, along with a currently operating one, and silently grieved the loss. I went to a protest rally, a hearing, and a weekend festival, all concerned with the social and ecological injustice of strip-mining.

That is, until I started dating Donnie. Through the fall and winter, all I knew of Donnie were the shy hellos he ventured at the store, and the embarrassed waves he gave when the unit Scout bumped past his house on the way up the hollow. He was a strip-miner—not one who owned a mine, but one who ran the heavy equipment necessary for boring the earth. He led a pretty monkist life at home with his ailing father and his mother—no brothers and sisters. By days he mined the earth and by nights ... well, I later learned that by nights (at least some nights; let's be modest) he wondered what I'd think about going out with him.

Eventually he got up enough nerve to ask Marlin to ask me if I would indeed ever consider going out with him.

I was embarrassed. "What are you, a matchmaker?" I laughed. In a second breath I added, "Why not?" After all, it might be interesting to get to know a "for real" miner.

Marlin told me everything he knew about Donnie and then added, "He's really a nice guy. It can't hurt."

Lawrence, Judi, and everyone was happy for me. I had a cold, though, and was scouring the unit for some "Contac," which brought loud guffaws from Dave and Marlin. "Contac . . . hee hee hee. Is that the way girls attract guys these days . . . hee hee hee."

Before I knew what was happening, I'd had three dates with Donnie and realized things had progressed beyond the "just friends," "might be interesting" arrangement I had bargained for.

It was the first time I'd ever dated a guy four years older than myself. He was so different from high school guys. In spite of his initial shyness, he soon took charge. Poised, responsible, experienced. I was impressed, queasy in the pit of my stomach, and scared. I knew I had to slow things down, lest either of us wind up getting badly hurt.

We were sitting at Jerry's Drive-In, waiting for Cokes on a date that was just to be a "drive into Hazard."

"Donnie," I began. "I really like you." His brown eyes smiled, but didn't say anything, hearing the "but" in my voice.

"But I think we better slow down a little, and not see each other quite so often. I really don't want—" I stumbled around, "a *romantic* involvement—I don't think."

"I suppose it could get complicated," he said reluctantly. "You don't know if you could live the rest of your life in these mountains, do you?"

I was stunned. He knew me better than I could have imagined.

"Well, I really would just like to be friends." I smiled, thinking of the flip way I had used that same line as an excuse to turn down a date weeks earlier with a 16-year-old who had asked me out. But this was sincere, and Donnie knew the difference, too.

"Fine. We'll just do things together. Have fun. I can show you around."

We sipped our Cokes awhile. "Does it ever bother you, being a strip-miner?" I asked.

"What do you mean?" I knew he was mainly stalling, to compose his answer.

"Well, you know, the way it ruins these mountains. The way people are cheated out of land. You *have* to know what the protestors are saying."

He smiled, shoved his car into gear, and pulled out of the drive-in. "Yeah. I have to make a living. Support my mom and dad. If you were me, would you rather go down in those mines, or work on top of the mountains?"

"But isn't there something else you can do?"

"Something that pays enough to support me and my folks, too? Without leaving these hills? Oh sure, I could migrate to Chicago or Detroit and get a good job and send the money home. And be called a hillbilly redneck just because of my accent and the car I drive."

"But doesn't it bother you to see whole tops of mountains stripped away? The trees? The creeks full of red water?" I pressed.

"Yes and no," he replied. "There are so many mountains around here and strip-mining scratches only a few. Besides, you know that the owners are now required to reseed and make the land usable again. Some have become nice recreation areas for folks—campgrounds and lakes, you know."

"Yeah, I know, although you know as well as I that their

efforts are mostly halfhearted at best," I countered.

"What I'd like to know is why the protestors come mostly from the colleges and from other areas. You don't see many of the people who are going to have to live and work here all their lives out at those rallies, do you?"

"Well, I don't know. I suppose not." I was beginning to realize I had been terribly presumptuous in trying to impose answers as a one-year import.

Donnie wasn't angry, just amusedly patient.

"I hope I didn't offend you. I just wanted to know what you think," I said finally.

"That's okay. It's not a perfect job, I know that. But you tell me what job is. At least around here. Most of the smart 'uns leave here for the cities. I guess I'm just not smart enough," he finished without self-pity.

"No, no," I protested. "I think it's great that you care enough for your folks to stay here and work hard at a job that is terribly dangerous, even though it's not down in a mine. I also think it's admirable that you don't spend your life hanging around the store getting drunk. What made you turn out differently than most of the guys around here?"

"I don't know," he looked at me gently. "Maybe the way I was raised. Maybe I'm just different. Maybe it's having you VSers always living nearby that keeps me from drinking." He was joking, a little.

I knew Donnie wasn't a Christian. Although he had strong morals and believed in God, he didn't profess to be something he wasn't, never having gone to church much. This was another reason I wanted to keep the relationship at a "just friends" level. I'd had it with trying to "convert" someone I was in love with. It mostly doesn't work.

But it was so nice to get out of the unit with someone other than the VSers. On one perfect March Sunday afternoon, Donnie and I took a drive some 50-to-60 miles to a natural bridge rock formation. We oohed and aahed at the sky, the trees, the rocks; we discovered a secret waterfall and took pictures of each other slurping the spray. We spotted a fire tower on a distant mountain and drove till we got to it, then panted to its top. We squeezed hands at the friendly croak of frogs and ended up at a small town drive-in for steak subs and french fries. As we rested tired muscles on the doorsteps that evening, Donnie said, "It's been a long time since I had such a good time."

"It was perfect," I agreed.

He kissed me quickly, once, and said, "Goodnight."

While one or two evenings a week were brightened by doing things with Donnie, nursery school, 4-H, and helping out as a teacher's aide in the first grade filled my days. Threading them all together was the nagging question of what do I do for an encore? VS may have temporarily stalled me from answering the "What should I do now?" question after high school—but it was not a place to escape life forever.

Although VS is touted as a noble thing to do for a year or two, it really was very secure. I generally didn't have to worry about getting fired, flunking out, or arguing with parents. We had only $15 a month allowance, but that is gravy when all your other needs are supplied. Oh, sure, the unit lived within a *budget,* but we always knew that if rent doubled or the car went bad or if the roof needed repair there was always headquarters to fall back on for funds.

I knew I wouldn't become a career VSer—entering another year of service to stall off the inevitable. The time had come to get on with my life, and I climbed mountains on Sunday afternoons to think, to warble operas, even occasionally to scream at God, like a four-year-old, "I want to

know your will for my life and I want to know it *now*."
Ironically, it wasn't often on the mountaintops that I got
nudges for direction, but in a letter from my oldest sister, in
casual conversation with unit members, or while sitting on
the courthouse steps on a snowy Saturday morning.

As Dave, Lawrence, and Judi reminisced about college
days frolics, it began to sound like fun. Lawrence assured me
that college was not only for those bent on being a nurse or
teacher—but good background for rounding out any personality. My sister Nancy wrote about the intangible ways
college had been "worth it" for her—the chance to examine
her faith objectively, her world attitude, her background. It
all started making sense for me. As I looked in the mirror one
evening I suddenly felt older, more mature. I knew that
waging my own youthful rebellion against the status quo
was not an issue anymore. Just because "everybody else does
it" no longer seemed like a good reason to stay out of
college. Just because some college-educated folks flashed
their education around like a young girl with a big new diamond, was not a good reason to write off all education.

But then $2,000 a year (1970 price!) was an awful lot of
money to spend rounding out my personality. Especially
when I had zero dollars in a bank account, and was earning
$15 a month. If I was supposed to go to college, why hadn't
God directed me at least to spend a year working at a paying
job instead of going into service?

What I didn't know was that, as usual, God had things
planned out far better than I could have ever imagined,
including a financial plan. And a career. But all that's
hindsight now. With foresight, all I could see was a small
flap lifting on the big picture that said, "Yes, college for a
year might be a good next step." But where? What major?
And what should I do about Donnie?

# 9

# The little gray church on Troublesome Creek

Sunday mornings were hectic at the unit, as in any household. Six adults had to get ready on time, which meant bathroom use was rationed carefully. Only more so because the unit ran its everlasting transportation service—picking up scattered passengers up this holler, down that creek. Often the unit drove two vehicles, and the lucky ones who got to go in the second van were able to leave much later and drive straight to church.

But the fellowship and communication that happened in the van was often as important as what happened at church. It was on these Sunday morning routes that I learned to know and care about Almina and Rebecca.

They were sisters who came regularly to church, which was admirable because not many teenagers did. Almina was the older with a wide face and grin, clear blue eyes, and wanting to be liked by the boys. Rebecca was less flirty, but with the same blue eyes and a consistently askew hemline.

"How come you not hitched up yet?" Almina asked me quizzically one morning.

"Well, I'm not really ready yet, I guess." I smiled. "Plus my father always said, 'You can't get married without a chance.'"

"Aw, go on. You've surely had plenty of chances. As pretty as you ..." she trailed off. Then, "How old is you, anyway."

"Just turned 19."

I could tell by her eyebrows that she thought I was ancient, that I'd be forever single, and what was wrong with me anyway?

I knew that it would not be unusual for her to be married by the time she was sixteen, and easily have three children by the time she was my age.

We picked up preschoolers, teenagers, middle-aged, and elderly, which sometimes took as much as an hour before and after church.

Orlo Fisher, the pastor, generally greeted everyone at the door of the little gray church. He'd ask about Almina's father and whether Joe had found a job yet. As VSers, we would come and go in the neighborhood—but as a family, they had chosen to stay and make this creek their home, their lifework. Sometimes I felt that my one-year commitment placed alongside their 20-to-40-year, or even lifetime, commitment was so frivolous—a youthful search for adventure and romance. No wonder VSers often feel there is so little they actually accomplish in a year or two—when long-term persons in mission make it their business to stay put in a place. I admired them for it, but they didn't look at it much differently than choosing to live in a middle-class suburb somewhere. It was where they went to Tupperware parties, and planted tulip bulbs and bought homes.

Orlo preached in high gear—at first I wanted to turn the volume down. Gradually I became as accustomed to it as the natives who considered it the sign of a good preacher. In a way, mountain worship services were as culturally different as walking into a black church in the inner city. At times, I wanted out of the same old ritual every Sunday morning— two songs, Scripture, prayer, another song, sermon. And when I led the singing or occasionally played the slightly off-key piano, I felt tied to use the same old songs.

One night in our room Louise, the new unit member, and I discussed our concerns for Almina and Rebecca, the church, and our spiritual lives in general. We fast discovered similar doubts: that even though we were doing what may have been considered very "religious," our spiritual lives were suffering. Away from the disciplines of home, I had to find new personal reasons for working at my spiritual growth. I no longer saw mom and dad read their Bible every morning, no family devotions at breakfast, no being at church every time it opened its doors for a meeting. Even though as a unit we were expected to participate in all the church functions, no one governed what we *thought* about during meetings, or enforced a devotional time.

And frankly, coming originally from a fairly large, professionally oriented congregation into this little mountain-oriented one wasn't easy. In fact, for the pastor to mold such a diverse congregation into a fellowship, meeting varying spiritual needs, had to be a real challenge.

As VSers we were expected to be resources for the church, teaching Sunday school as needed, leading worship or singing, providing transportation, doing visitation, and supporting the youth group activities. The VS unit also carried on some activities independent of the church's official functions, but with some of the same community persons. So it took a real effort by everyone to keep communication open, to share facilities and beliefs while sometimes approaching mission and outreach from different viewpoints.

In addition, for the most part the community people had little understanding of these somewhat plain-looking people whose women wore little white caps and whose men didn't have to go to Vietnam. Why did the VSers mysteriously come in on a Greyhound and a year or two later leave again? Didn't they have homes? Roots?

"I feel like such a hypocrite! It's a farce. No one ever looks like they really mean the words they're singing," I complained.

"I know," Louise joined in. "It seems like if we sang choruses or more current songs it would be more appropriate for the youth group."

"I really miss the close fellowship I had with the kids at home. There just doesn't seem to be any life here," I continued.

We ranted on, trying to blame in turn the youth, the unit, the minister. Suddenly we stopped, and I knew that she knew I felt as guilty as she did. Louise led us both in a spontaneous prayer asking for forgiveness and guidance. I could continue blaming external symptoms if I wanted to, but the problem really was with me and my attitude.

I recalled that just the past Sunday the sermon had been particularly meaningful and I hadn't even thanked the pastor, like an ungrateful leper. I was so used to writing a mental critique as a minister preached that I wasn't even allowing the Spirit of God to touch me. Maybe if I started having a more positive attitude and concentrated on singing the words myself with meaning, then I would be able to worship God the only way he can be worshiped anyway—"in spirit and in truth."

A change in attitude didn't produce a perfect church, but then I had never belonged to a perfect church. In communion services with the believers there, I sipped from the joint communion cup and tried not to think about germs. In the foot washing service, where church members wash each other's feet in remembrance of Jesus' act at the Last Supper, I washed a woman's feet that really needed washing. It was such a switch from my girlhood church where everyone scrubbed their feet spotless and neatly trimmed their toenails on the Saturday night before foot washing, which turned the ceremony into one with no practical purpose! For the first time I realized the lowliness of the service Jesus performed—the feet he washed that night were dirty, smelly, grimy.

As the woman padded back to the bench to roll up her stockings, I felt more in touch with my own humanity. My pompous, self-righteous desire to give the impression my feet didn't ever get smelly had been punctured by her earthiness and honesty. Talk about object lessons! Talk about God breaking through to us in spite of ourselves! I began to look for more ways to listen to God, and to be responsive to his Word. I carried on extensive conversation with myself—mostly in the woods, or in my journal, where I attempted to deepen my walk with him. I also realized I needed other people in my walk, and began to reach out to the unit more.

Unit discussions on spiritual matters were rarely planned or orchestrated. And because they were spontaneous, they seemed both alive with God's presence and active Holy Spirit.

We agonized both over how to live and how to verbalize our witness, and how the alternatives to military service available to guys my age were not very attractive.

We talked about the growing Jesus People movement, of whether it would last or was just a fad. And hadn't they created their own "established religion," where jeans, stringy hair, and raised hands praising the Lord were the rule, thereby boxing in God and everyone else?

My best days were those filled with activity, topped off by gathering in the living room to talk, pray, sing, laugh, or cry. The close unit life I had hoped for was beginning. I was learning to know the others well enough to *care* about them. And to like myself enough that I felt secure in just being myself—joking, crazy sometimes, human. I even gained the courage to admit to the others why I loved long walks in the woods and hills that ringed us on all sides: that it was my way of dealing with myself and with God.

On my walks I pondered whether Jesus was ever 19, and going in a million ways at once. Did he always know he was the Messiah, or did he doubt and wonder and need to go away to think sometimes, too? I wondered why there was nothing in the Bible about him at 19 and hoped that it meant that maybe I'd have things more together by the time I was 30.

The mountaintops always gave new perspective for life on Troublesome Creek. Once I perched where I could see the entire little community of Ary. To my left was the school—looking very old and unexciting, yet solid and stable. Traditional. Teacherly. In front of me were the picturesque cottages with smoke curling from chimneys. Romantic. Homelike.

And to the right was a hill, one that I hadn't explored. It was like all the other hills, yet higher and more intriguing because I didn't know its secrets yet. Could I reject both the teacher and wife options that everyone said I fit so well in hopes that the unexplored hill held something better? Something more in line with all that God had in mind when he created me?

It was certainly more risky—to travel new territory than go with the acceptable careers of teacher/homemaker. But somehow that "other hill" was the one I longed for.

# 10

# Signs of spring

Spring mornings on Troublesome Creek were invigorating. The fog slowly burned off to reveal tender new green shoots on trees, perky daffodils, and often a piercing blue sky. On such days, I kissed the air and echoed good morning to a neighbor, beginning my rounds with a peace and fulfillment that made me wish I could stay in VS forever.

I helped my nursery schoolers observe the various signs of spring. We took walks and I pointed out crocuses, robins, and new grass. Over the weekend they were to watch for spring signs, too.

Monday morning Davey was ready. "I saw a sign of spring!"

"Oh, really!" I was pleased. "And what was it?"

"Well, it was at the Magic Mart (discount store) and it was sticking in the grass on a stick and it was wood and it said, 'Spring Sale.' "

I couldn't help smiling and agreeing with Davey that, yes,

that was definitely a "sign" of spring—in more ways than one.

Earlier in the year, in February, I started helping as a teacher's aide in the first grade every afternoon. I began assisting slower readers with sophisticated little gadgets designed to encourage them to want to read. It was a relief to have some structure to my day that I didn't have to prepare for—no home ec demonstration to plan or nursery school busy work to ready.

In the first-grade room, it bothered me that the brighter pupils seemed to be seated toward the front of the room, and the slower ones in the back. There was one boy who seemed almost blind and another who needed glasses so badly I was sure it was keeping him behind in his work. There were little boys with bad crushes on their teacher's aide, who scrambled to sit beside me at the reading table. And there were bright, pigtailed little girls who knew all the answers and wore pretty, ironed dresses, as well as girls with messy hair and torn hand-me-down cheap jeans and tops. For the most part, the children didn't seem to notice whether their friends' clothes were neatly ironed or badly torn.

One day on the playground I noticed a tattered Kelly standing off to the side with tears in her eyes. I stooped and asked, "What's wrong, Kelly?"

(Sniff, sniff) "Sherry pushed" (sniff, sniff) "me."

"Oh. Did she do it on purpose?"

She solemnly shook her head no.

"Okay. Let's find Sherry."

We did and I asked if she knew she had pushed Kelly and if she didn't want to tell Kelly she was sorry.

She did and both girls looked at me with smiles—then at each other. "Wanna play?" And they were off, skipping and holding hands.

For my adolescent junior high girls, problems were not resolved so easily.

I was usually in my classroom early and one or more girls would come and I'd find out about the fusses their parents were having or about how "Belinda thinks she's so pretty now that she's a cheerleader."

One day before any girls arrived, I started thinking about what a dump the place was when I first saw it—cold and dark with tables and chairs piled all over, and footballs and horseshoes and even a voting machine. And I remembered washing windows and sweeping the floor again and again until not so much dirt and sand came up through the floorboards. I had stacked things in neat piles (no hope of clearing them out) and finally the principal had even turned on some heat for the room. It had my touch.

I looked at the sewing machines, and thought of how we had started without even any scissors or pins and I got the girls to buy sewing kits for themselves.

And suddenly, I think I knew part of why I had come. If I hadn't been there, this little outbuilding for the physical education department (or P.E. shack, as the girls called it) would probably still be just a P.E. shack, with piles of equipment and with no one's special touch.

Maybe I wouldn't save the world, but for one year I would save a P.E. shack.

As the year went on, I started realizing it wasn't home ec teaching that I enjoyed so much, but the conversations with the girls. In fact, I pondered Bible verses like, "Life is more than clothes and food," and wondered how I could ever reconcile that with teaching girls to be concerned about making clothes and food. It was immature reasoning, but at least it led me even further away from pursuing teaching as a career.

If I wasn't going to be a teacher, what *could* I do? The neat symbolism from my Sunday walk—where I had decided boldly to go for that "other hill"—seemed hopelessly vague in the clear light of Monday noon. Didn't I need to know what that other hill was, before I went to college? A straight-laced freshman adviser would certainly not understand my lovely symbolism. I thought it would be so convenient if I could just sit down and write a letter to God and have him write back and tell me exactly what his will was for my life. Instead, I had to write to registrars and personnel departments and look at my bank account and put all those together to find out what he was saying.

Then I went on a fast. Now, I always thought people who fasted were a little overzealous spiritually. But I wanted to lose weight anyway, and since many days I was on my own for lunch, I decided that I could discreetly fast by not eating anything after breakfast until suppertime. Every time I thought about being hungry, I prayed for God's guidance for my life.

Call it coincidence or Providence, things happened that week besides losing weight. Out of the blue I received a call from the financial aid director at the college I was considering, but hadn't applied to because I didn't have the money. So how had he gotten my name?

"Well, I was talking to a fellow the other day who said he went to high school with you and that maybe you'd be interested, but he knew you didn't have the money."

I knew immediately who he was talking about. Good old Chuck. We had been high school and church friends—purely platonic—and had exchanged a friendly round of letters once or twice during the year.

The financial aid man talked like they could make me an offer too good to refuse. The next step was to send in my ap-

77

plication, and have my folks fill out some income statements.

If I went away to college, what would I do about Donnie? We had gotten to the point of liking each other very much. One evening we even agreed, very businesslike, that (1) we both had traits the other admired, (2) it *could* grow into love, and (3) we were as "different as daylight from dark" (Donnie's phrase).

I also knew that what I felt with him was so different from high school romances. Here was a man, 23, obviously ready for marriage, with none of the need to run around showing off his car or girl. I knew that unless he really became a Christian, I couldn't continue seeing him, and at times tried to convince myself that I would be copping out of "witnessing" to him if we broke up. At my request, the night before Easter we went to a nearby revival meeting, where a youth worker from a city oohed and aahed the audience by tales of derelict drug addicts. In spite of the tactics, God seemed to speak to Donnie anyway, and that night we had a good talk about what it means to be a Christian. I was glad that he had enough integrity that he wasn't about to fake a conversion just to please me.

I put off breaking off, mostly because I knew and he knew that it was more or less inevitable, and meanwhile we both enjoyed the companionship. He helped me feel like at least I partially understood one person on Troublesome Creek, which gave me courage to reach out to others.

I even grew brave enough to take Caroline Williams up on her standing offer to come and have supper with her. It was her mother's birthday, and it would just be her family, but I knew Caroline would feel special if I came.

So I took the Scout Saturday afternoon and lumbered over deep red ruts back to her home hidden farthest back

"Wolf Pen" holler. Winter snows and spring rains had made the road almost impassable, and I knew that the persons who peeked out from the scattered houses along the way wondered what that silly young girl from the unit was up to now. Many of the mountain women didn't drive at all, never mind all alone in a four-wheel drive with a stick shift. Usually Judi and I or Louise went visiting together, but this was an evening just for me.

Caroline's 25-year-old sister, Midge, came home from work and whipped out a supper with such efficiency it left me breathless. She whacked up a chicken and put it on the old woodburning cookstove to fry, peeled potatoes for later mashing, shred some cabbage for cole slaw, beat up dumplings and cornbread batter. Then from the fridge she warmed up a pot of shucky beans and soup beans—all within 30 minutes. I *timed* her. She asked one of the boys to get fresh water from the well, and put the bucket on the table while setting it with an odd assortment of plates, and one fork to complete each setting. Of course, I had to taste everything—and it *was* delicious. I wondered how I had ever dared to think I could teach Caroline anything about cooking.

On another visit to a home with potential kindergarten students for next year, I realized just how good Caroline and her family had it, comparatively. There was a little five-year-old boy—eyes painfully dulled and scared. He was followed around by a two-year-old diaperless sister; there were two children playing in the "yard"—a dirt area surrounded by more dirt. And the mother held another baby on her knees. The house was the bleakest I'd ever seen—plain wood floors and walls, an old sofa, and the barest of kitchen equipment. Chickens from the yard wandered in the back door, and the smell of urine was so strong I breathed through my mouth the whole time we were there.

We talked about little Robert needing kindergarten and the mother was kind and agreeable, but we knew and she knew she would never follow up on it. Where was the energy to get a five-year-old ready to go to kindergarten at some nice church? Where would the money come from to keep Robert smelling clean enough? Sometimes even well-intentioned help in the form of a kindergarten was not enough to help those on society's bottom rung—those who'd lost all hope for things ever being any different. I felt so helpless and empty—for their futures that would never be, for the wasted potential of human lives. Caroline and her family would make it—maybe not by society's standards, but they were *family*—together, gardening, enjoying a simple but peaceful way of life. I wasn't so sure about this family.

On our way back to the apartment, Judi commented that Troublesome Creek was higher than normal—even for spring. It had rained a lot that week, and more was forecast for the weekend. The water in the stream was already brown and rushing fast, floating some debris along with it.

By morning I was called out of bed to "Come look at the school."

"The school?" I wondered. The creek was a good 300 yards away from the school. What could be the matter?

But the entire schoolyard was under brown ugly water. For the first time in my life I knew the fear of watching water rise beyond its banks, not knowing how or when it would stop. Down the center of the flooding waters it seemed that all of Kentucky's trash went on parade: bottles, fenders, toilet paper, limbs, brush, cans, boxes, boards.

The roar of the river was with us all morning, kind of like the tumult my life was in. I waited and watched the river, and wondered when things would get back to normal.

Somebody said the river had already started to recede. How did anyone know? I didn't trust it, and began to understand how Troublesome had earned its name.

By noon I knew the report was right. It *was* going down, and had already started to strew its souvenirs amidst the low branches and bushes along its banks—cans and paper trash—making the brush look like cheap gaudy Christmas trees. But what if more rain came that day or night? I could only guess at the shape of Caroline's road, or little Robert's play "yard."

After the river went down, I couldn't wait to talk to Donnie, to find out how it had felt to sit at river bottom level and wonder how far it would come.

"Oh, it wasn't bad." He gave me his slow smile. We were sitting in his car. "Just one of those things. Happens most every year."

"It was exciting. I've never been around a flood before," I said, like a school girl. "But I don't know if I'd want to live where my home could be threatened any year by a flood like that."

"Well, it's home. The mountain people don't leave home just because the water rises," he reminded me.

I thought of the cemetery I had climbed to with Winky, and how that was part of the reason he gave me that cemeteries were plotted so high in the mountains.

Donnie was studying me. "I'm not sure you could ever really be happy here anyway."

My heart flipped. Was this the opening I was waiting for? Was he baiting me, testing me?

"I don't know either."

"You'd be too tied down. I just can't see you that way."

I looked at him. "Oh, Donnie," I said putting my arms around him, "you've been a great friend—and I'd like to keep on being friends for the rest of my time here ... but ... it's just not fair for me to tie you down with false hopes, you being 23 and all." The words tumbled out in half sentences. I never was very good at such scenes.

He held me for a few minutes. "I'm sorry it won't work out. Always remember, I think you're very pretty."

I wanted to kiss him, just once for good-bye, but he made no move. I jumped from his car, quickly, before I could change my mind, and felt like both rejoicing and crying. He had made it so easy for me, and I knew it was the right decision. But yet I couldn't help hurting, more for him than for me.

Later that week his father entered the hospital. And if that wasn't enough, Marlin said Donnie had a potentially fatal accident the same week on the strip mine. His dozer had turned over. I remembered how shaken Donnie had been by the death of a strip miner just two months earlier in a similar accident. Had we broken up at the wrong time? Or maybe it was the right time, because I would not have had the guts to do it for some weeks after his accident. Even if it had been the right move, I hurt for him and prayed. A friend had once told me to just pray that "God will put his arms around the one you care about."

As I sat on the porch and looked toward his house across the creek bottom, it seemed like God put his arms around me too. Swallows were swooping the freshness of new-mown grass, and crickets chirped their joy of the wet warmth. Up and down the holler I could see lights coming on. Troublesome Creek had receded to its old lines. As I memorized the pureness of the sky edged with the velvety hills, I wanted to shout, "God, you have made everything beautiful!"

Instead, an old jalopy came screeching out of the holler.

# 11

# Like icing on the cake

V S is the only place I know of where you feel noble shelling peas. Between the close of nursery school and the beginning of day camp for which I was to be codirector, there was a change-of-pace week where I worked in the garden, prepared to teach summer Bible school, and gathered craft ideas for day camp.

As day spilled into evening, a handful of kids and I played softball at the elementary school diamond, and a little boy named Wayne developed a crush on me. He called me several times a day to check out whether I would be playing softball that evening. As the firefly-studded dusks settled in the holler, I could hear children playing half a mile away. Whiffs of family camping trips came floating from my memory.

One afternoon there was a knock at the unit door. Judi called from her room, "Melodie, could you get it?" I didn't think anything strange about that, since by this time she was a very eight months pregnant, and taking an afternoon rest. Only later did I find out that she and the rest of the unit had kept a secret that I discovered when I opened the door. There stood my sister Linda!

"How on earth ... how'd you get here ... how long can you stay? I scarcely knew what to ask first. It seemed so strange to transplant this face from home to this world that had been my very own. Finally, I had "family" to show off. Although I'd always loved the visits of other unit members' families, in some small way substituting them for my own, I always felt a little jealous too—that their families lived so close by, and had enough money to travel.

Linda was on her way from college to home, she said, and had traveled here with her roommate from college. She would be taking a flight out two days later, and thought she could spend the time with me.

"Oh, I wish you could stay longer, but I guess this is better than nothing." I wanted to show her everything all at once, to help her sample in two short days what it had taken me nine months to absorb.

I knew of no better place to let her savor a real Kentucky home than at Caroline Williams' home on Wolf Pen. They insisted we stay for chicken and mashed potatoes and shucky beans again, and I nudged Linda during supper to make sure she noted the water pail on the table.

I still envied Linda's ability to laugh so deeply, to captivate almost everyone she met with her charisma. But it was a different envy now, one with pride attached that this was my sister. Now that I had my own job, a circle of admiring 4-Hers, unit members who knew my own special brand of humor and personality, I could accept her with hers. What freedom from self it was to finally let go of the creeping old bad feelings I seemed to grow up with. Not that they wouldn't ever haunt me again in low moments. But it felt good to feel that maybe this was what growing up was all about—entering new levels of awareness and relationships.

The time to take her to the airport soon came, but she said she had looked at her ticket wrong and the flight was really an hour later, and why not go shoot a few rounds of basketball over at the school? I was nervous about not getting to the airport on time, but for some reason didn't insist on leaving when I thought we should. It was really like old times shooting ball with her, and we reminisced about the high school game in which the coach had run out of substitutes and I had to play the whole game and I kept passing off to her and whispering, "I think I'm gonna be sick." We laughed and dribbled and feinted and played so hard that at first I dismissed the man, woman, and tall lanky boy walking slowly toward us in the deserted old cove. They could have been just another mountain family trudging homeward. But slowly I realized they looked different—too dressed up and familiar.

"Mom! Dad! Terry!" I took off shouting, and was soon hugging all three. "I can't believe it! First Linda. Now you guys!" Linda, of course, had prearranged for mom and dad to meet her here, so the flight home was nothing more than a ruse to make things plausible.

"I feel like I better confess all my fibs," Linda was saying, and mom added seriously, "Well, you'd *better*."

"That's why I wanted to play ball this afternoon—to keep us here to meet mom and dad!" she explained.

"Ohh!" I groaned. "I should have suspected something. How could I be so dumb?" I looked at my watch. "We . . . we would never have made it!"

We all laughed.

"Well—did the unit know about this, too?"

They all nodded, brimming with smiles.

"Oh, you guys," was all I could say to hold the happiness I felt—to think of my two families scheming to surprise me so completely. I felt more whole than I had in months, like finally my two lives were brought together. My past now connected to the present, and if *that* was possible, then maybe everything would connect in the future, too. I knew it had been difficult for dad to get away from the farm just then, and what a financial burden it was.

We packed a week's worth of adventures into a too-short weekend, going on a picnic, a mountain climb, shopping, a worship service, and lots of time to just be together. I enjoyed the warm glow of knowing that someone cared enough to drive 700 miles out of their way to see me. The only one missing was my married sister and her family.

It turned out to be the high I needed to rush headlong into the demands of the rest of the summer. The codirector of day camp was a college student in Kentucky for the summer, who turned out to be my second cousin, Diane Miller. We met at a seminar designed to orient summer students to the needs and people of Appalachia. We shyly looked each other over, remembering, I suppose, the last family reunion we'd both been to. We were both ten and she was chubby and I was pigtailed and plain. Now she was a striking blond with a figure to match, and at first I was scared I wouldn't like my own relative. But her disarming, natural smile and welcome made me feel like we were both ten and plain again.

We soon forgot our common blood in the flurry of finalizing day camp details. Now our bond was: would the girls like us as well as the vivacious creative VSer they'd had last year whom we'd heard so much about? Would we be able to keep them from getting bored, bitten by rattlesnakes, and from spending all their money on soda pop and chips?

We directed three camps for three different age-groups, running two weeks each. Besides planning, organizing, and carrying out the activities, we took turns driving the van for an hour each morning and evening to pick up and deliver the girls. Sometimes I thought that "VS" stood for Van Service—it was such an integral part of everything we did. Sometimes it seemed like we were being taken advantage of . . . but I realized it was precisely a lack of transportation that kept many of these people isolated in their hollers.

My legs often ached when the last girl was dropped at the foot of her swinging bridge; we were sweaty and depleted from giving all day long. During the first two weeks of day camp, we also taught summer Bible school, and canned beans for next year's VSers. Some nights we worked till midnight, not realizing that piling summer days full with a job, summer Bible school, and midnight canning sessions wouldn't necessarily end with VS.

What about the rest of what I was doing—would scrimping on clothes, making do without luxuries, and trying actively to know and understand my neighbors end with VS?

"I'm so hungry for a Big Mac that I think I'll go on a year-long fast-food binge when I get out," I joked with Dave one evening.

"And buy a fancy sports car that guzzles gas," he kidded.

"And order the biggest banana split with a whole *row* of maraschino cherries . . . ."

"And live in a mansion with a pool and servants and own 15 strip mines to rip off the poor . . . ."

It was pure fantasy, the kind of exaggerating two teenagers do after a date.

I began to understand that what had brought me into VS was not a superficial belief in looking out for the needs of others and living simply. It was ingrained in me from my childhood—a fact brought home to me by the example of my over-70 aunt and uncle who joined the unit for two weeks in June to help out with Bible school. My aunt was a career Bible school teacher—sometimes volunteering her time to teach 6-to-8 weeks out of the summer, from the inner city of Chicago to the upper peninsula of Michigan. During the day, she didn't just sit around knitting either. She pitched in with the canning, the housework, with visiting the neighbors. Even at her age, she was like a sponge, wanting to soak up all the culture she could from these people she had taught among so often.

A brother of one of my day campers was tragically killed in a car accident while my aunt and uncle were there. The burial was to be high on a mountainside and Susie joined me in the Scout to attend "because I've never been to a mountain funeral." The road was little more than a trail, and with recent rains the mud was deep and treacherous. She held onto her seat and her breath as I braced the steering wheel to keep it on the trail.

When the funeral was over, I tried to turn the Scout around on the narrow road, without much success. A guy about 22 volunteered to try, so my aunt got out and I sat in the front.

"I'm Casey Jones," he flashed a quick grin, his blue eyes showing he knew women found him attractive.

I had vaguely heard of him from the day camp girls.

"I'm Melodie Miller."

"Oh, yes, from Rachel's store." He didn't waste any time. "Are you married?"

I almost laughed. "Uh, well *no*." It was as if he was used to having to ask . . . or maybe he thought I looked rather old not to be married.

"Go out much?"

"Oh, some. When I get a chance."

"You mean, you *do* date," he clarified.

"Well, yes." I wondered then at some of the misconceptions the people must have had about Mennonites and what they do and don't do.

"Well, would you go out with me tonight?"

I flushed. No one had ever tried to pick me up like that before. Or was it a pickup? I mean, my aunt was standing right outside and . . . he was nice and nice looking.

"Well, I'll have to think about it."

"Okay," but he hopped out of the Scout without getting my phone number. I was sure Susie could tell from my blush what had gone on.

"Well, that was sure interesting," she said and I nodded, but not about the funeral. There was a wild streak in me that wanted him to call, that wanted to say who cares about being a nice girl who does only the expected things. Since I'd be leaving in a month or two anyway, why not have one last romantic fling and get to know another Kentucky fellow?

I lay in bed a night or two later wondering why he hadn't called yet, guessing he never would. Suddenly I became aware of something moving on the screen right at the head of my bed. It was smooth and skinny and shiny in the moonlight.

My stomach curled. A snake. Not more than 12 inches from my head—although there *was* a screen between me and it. I grabbed a robe and called for Marlin, who killed it and said it was a copperhead.

I felt crawly the rest of that night. The remainder of the summer in day camp when we picked blackberries up along an old strip mine, I carried a hoe and looked more for snakes than I did for blackberries. But the girls busily picked and we had enough to make 10 pints of blackberry jelly the next day at camp—one for each girl to take home and two left over.

One day each week we took the girls 45 minutes away to Buckhorn "Lake"—a man-made reservoir. But you'd have thought we were going to the beach. It was the high point of day camp for the girls—and to be truthful, a nice break for the leaders as well. It was one day when nothing other than swimming was on the agenda and we could work on our tans—although we did worry about keeping track of everyone. The responsibility of 8-to-10 lives resting in my hands as we curved around the mountains was never completely forgotten.

Each day I thanked God for safety, and looked to him for strength—sometimes literally. One morning I woke early with the kind of splitting headache that I would have cut classes for in high school. But here were girls depending on me. I took two aspirin and breathed a prayer as I crawled back in bed for another half hour. The headache left—not a miracle by most people's standards, considering pills and extra rest. But *I* interpreted it as a sign of God's help in my life that day.

Just like the fact that I was going to Eastern Mennonite College in the fall. Nothing miraculous. People do it every fall. But a year earlier I would have said: "Highly unlikely." "No money." "No major." "It's just not for me."

Somehow I had gotten in a unit with three EMC graduates, plus one who was dating an EMC student. My coleader for day camp was from EMC. In the course of a year I had ruled out marriage for the time being, and the financial aid officer had worked out a plan too good to refuse.

I still didn't know what I wanted to become—not that I didn't frequently beg God to tell me. Wasn't I and VS a failure if I couldn't say exactly what I wanted to do after a whole year to think it over? Why did I have to be so wishy-washy, and interested in so many different things?

In spite of my questions, I had seen enough of how God worked things out in the past that mostly I felt as peaceful as a Kentucky summer evening. As the summer ripened, I felt deeply satisfied—rich as icing on a cake.

I attended an occasional square dance, went to an anti-strip-mining rally, chatted on porches, talked with one of my older Bible school students about what it meant to be a pacifist, and went hiking with a friend from day camp. The unit was invited to a "memorial dinner," which was a service and meal held each year upon the anniversary of the death of a loved one. I had never heard of such an odd celebration, and thought it unhealthy for mourners to weep and wail as loudly as if the person had just died. But on second thought, wasn't this one more example of their acceptance of the fates of life—that death is remembered and celebrated, like an odd birthday party? It was at times like the memorial service that I knew one year was so laughably short to begin to understand and appreciate a culture so complex as the one in Appalachia.

# 12

# Not the end, but a beginning

By the first of August, mentally I had already left Kentucky and was rehearsing my life as a college freshman. It was easy to find myself not really caring anymore, like—Why worry about doing major unit chores? We'll let that for the new unit hostess.

Judi and Lawrence had finished their terms a little early to go "home" and have their baby. I was also leaving a few weeks early to spend a week at home before starting college. I worried that the VS administrators would be disappointed with my "lack of commitment." But they assured me that they were in favor of higher education and that they often granted such requests. An honorable early discharge!

So with the Brennemans already gone and two new members who joined the unit in July, it seemed like my year was already over. The new unit members were delightful additions, of course, but the old camaraderie of 11 months of living together wasn't there.

I was dreading the next few weeks, too, because I'd always hated good-byes. Because it's hard to sum up in a few succinct words all that a person means, and I often resort to mumbling something nondescript like, "It was so good to know you." At 19, I hadn't gone through enough good-byes yet to realize that saying good-bye meaningfully is a real art, and that everybody knows good-bye is a lousy way to end a relationship.

I also knew that good-bye meant new hellos were coming. Soon I would have to start all over in the difficult job of feeling at home in a new place. The prospect of making all new friends at college looked scary. I still had the notion that all college graduates spouted sociological jargon about the foibles of human behavior—and I wanted no part of that. Could I keep my rather simple outlook of just wanting to equip myself to love, serve, and be a help to other people?

Donnie must have heard through the Troublesome News Network that I was leaving. One perfect evening he walked over just to talk. The night was unusually nippy for early August and the moon was out. In effect he told me he loved me. I looked at him, knowing that he would probably soon be married with two kids and a parakeet, and for a moment I wished it would be me. But only a moment. The hills could not hold me now. They would have closed in on me, like sinking sand, suffocating its victim.

Knowing that college was my next step filled me with the sweet peace that comes only after earnestly seeking God's will. I had wanted him to map out my whole life miraculously. Instead he gave me a nudge for one year at a time.

As Donnie walked back to his home across the holler, I watched another group of guys wasting away the summer night under the light pole. They looked so idle—just smoking, drinking, sitting. Suddenly I knew that what I had accomplished in one short year was so little. How could they stand the everlasting nothingness of their lives? Or was that just my value judgment, one that would be different later when *I* was tied down to a job/TV/sleep routine? Was such a routine any more meaningful? The worst feeling was not even knowing how to pray for them.

As I pondered that, I remembered the Jesus People paper that someone had shoved at me at Buckhorn Lake that day. They seemed to have all the answers to living out wasted lives, but I suspected a fad. It seemed like the dirty jeans and hip talk and simple guitar songs were as much status symbols in the Jesus People Movement as dress suits and four-part hymns were to the established church. If what they had inside was for real, if it was something missing from my spiritual life, I wanted it. But not if the counter-culture Jesus movement was just another passing fad.

I longed to talk to dad about his views on it. He was always so sensible about things, yet single-minded in devotion to God. Even as I longed for his opinion on the movement, I knew that wouldn't suffice for me now. Religion was easy when you had your folks directing you on how often to go to church, on who to believe and who was a quack. Now I would have to decide for myself. I did have enough faith in my intelligence and common sense to know that somehow I'd make the right decision, and felt a sudden rush of gladness that my parents had equipped me to do that. And if I made mistakes, well, they'd be there—maybe looking on with scowls and worried brows and prayers, but *there*. It felt good to be going home to parents like that.

I called on favorite neighbors for "one last time." Rachel was still quilting, and sad that once again a unit member was leaving.

"Why, we hardly get to know you, and then you leave."

"I know," I said. "It's not that we want to leave, but we come here with that in mind—to leave at the end of a year or two years."

I squeezed her worn, smooth hand with veins marking her years. "So it's not that we're leaving because we don't like it. That's just the way VS is."

My excuse was lame but she was generous, both with praise for my work and for all the Mennonite young people who had passed through the unit in general. I knew enough to take it with a pinch of salt. Being nice to a person's face and then more candid behind his back was not, in the mountains, two-faced. It was simply chivalry, another remnant from the days of lords and manors in England, I suppose. It was also a way of maintaining a certain reserve, the right to privacy.

Rachel was completely sincere, but I *knew* that not *everyone* in the community loved me and would miss me. To some I had been barely visible—a quiet mouse of a girl who was a long time in letting down her guard to be friendly. Perhaps in that I was a little like the traditional mountain person—wanting to maintain a circle of private space. But I also knew that I would have to continue to work at being more outgoing and friendly.

For those were the most rewarding times of VS—not when I was squirreled away in my room writing impressions in a journal, nor when exalting in God's handiwork on a solitary climb in the hills. It wasn't when I sat mute and stonelike in the van, bouncing to and from school or day camp lost in private thoughts.

But rather, fulfillment came when I took the time and dared to take Ernest, the blind man, by the hand and say, "Hi, Ernest. This is Melodie. How *are* you today?" Or when

I dared to tell my roommate how I really felt about church, or about Donnie, or about the other unit members. Or the times we got just plain silly as a unit and I was surprised to find people actually laughing at my jokes.

Those were the times that would live in my not-perfect memory. Time would erase or block out the bad feelings, with only a tattered old journal to remind me of them.

I thought I had entered VS to maybe change the world of a few persons. I ended up changing myself.

I thought I would be able to help people see how they could move closer to the middle-class model by just shaping up here and there. A few conversions sprinkled in would have even been nice.

I ended up discovering that *people* aren't the ones who bring about spiritual change in others. Only God can do that. Oh, I could talk and pray and be a friend, but only God could move people to accept the Jesus I was attempting to serve. And with poetic justice, I learned that I was really the one "standin' in the need of prayer."

As I boarded the familiar old Greyhound that would carry me back to the land of shopping malls and suburban sprawl, I wanted to reach out and cling to the mountains and creeks and hollers that wound beside the road. I wanted to keep everything just like it was, and yet take it with me. But my rational side knew that was as impossible as trying to keep change and the worst sides of progress from slowly infecting these hills. Kentucky was changing all right, but not because of a few VSers trying to live in communities working their hearts out.

Kentucky would never be the same.

I would never be the same, either. And I wasn't sure whether to rejoice or cry.

**Melodie Miller Davis** works half time for Mennonite Board of Missions (MBM) Media Ministries in Harrisonburg, Virginia, as a staff writer for radio programs and promotional materials. She also raises two daughters, Michelle and Tanya, with her husband, Stuart, and does free-lance writing. From 1975-1981 she worked full time with MBM as a producer and writer.

She graduated from Eastern Mennonite College, Harrisonburg, with a BA in 1975, after studying a year at the University of Barcelona, Spain.

Born at Sarasota, Florida, she spent her growing-up years near Goshen, Indiana, in a Mennonite farm family of two sisters and one brother. In 1969, her family moved to northern Florida, prior to her entering the MBM Voluntary

Service program at Ary, Kentucky in 1970, where the experiences of this book happened.

The Davises are members of Trinity Presbyterian Church in Harrisonburg, a house-church-based congregation actively involved in community outreach.

Melodie is also the author of *For the Next Nine Months: Meditations for Expectant Mothers* (Zondervan) and *Working, Mothering and Other Minor Dilemmas* (Word Books).

# Voluntary Service Agencies

Readers of this book who are thinking of investing a year or two of their lives in voluntary service assignment may contact one or more of the following offices:

*Mennonite Board of Missions, Mennonite Church*
Consider using your gifts and talents to respond to human need as you invite others to faith in Jesus Christ during a one- or two-year assignment with Mennonite Board of Missions. Placements are available in nursing and health services, home repair, social work, education, involvement with programs assisting the elderly and disabled, and various community ministries serving the poor, powerless, and oppressed. Contact MBM Personnel Counselor, Box 370, Elkhart, IN 46515. Phone (219) 294-7523.

*Eastern Mennonite Board of Missions and Charities, Mennonite Church*
Eastern Mennonite Board of Missions and Charities' voluntary service program seeks to involve individuals who are interested in sharing their talents and skills in a holistic Christian ministry, motivated by the call of Christ and his example. Assignments are located along the East Coast, working at peace and justice issues, hospital work, construction, child care, youth work, and other assignments which deal with the needs that are

present in the community of that particular household. For information call or write: Discipleship Ministries, Voluntary Service Office, Oak Lane and Brandt Blvd., Salunga, PA 17538. Phone (717) 898-2251.

*Rosedale Mennonite Missions, Conservative Mennonite Conference*

Rosedale Mennonite Missions provides opportunity for volunteers, committed to Christ and the church, to serve in voluntary service assignments in the United States, Latin America, and Europe. Assignments include youth work, child care, housing, nursing homes, rehabilitation of handicapped persons, nursing, teaching, and agriculture. Contact Rosedale Mennonite Missions, 9920 Rosedale M. C. Rd., Irwin, OH 43029. Phone (614) 857-1366.

*Commission on Home Ministries, General Conference Mennonite Church*

Mennonite Voluntary Service assists local communities in confronting social, economic, political, and spiritual problems. Mennonite Voluntary Service needs people of varied backgrounds, skills, and interests to participate in service ministries from community organizing to housing repair, from child care to peacemaking, from youth work to ministries with aging, from teaching to prison ministries. For information and application contact Mennonite Voluntary Service, Box 347, Newton, KS 67114. Phone (316) 283-5100.

*Office of Christian Service, Mennonite Brethren Church*

The primary purpose of Mennonite Brethren Christian Service is to "Help Build the Church." Volunteers of all ages serve in Christian institutions or in areas of human needs while helping young or emerging churches. The address for information is Mennonite Brethren Christian Service, 4812 E. Butler Ave., Fresno, CA 93727. Phone (209) 251-8681.

*Brethren in Christ Missions*

High school or college graduates of all ages may apply for voluntary service positions with Brethren in Christ Missions in institutional programs, retirement homes, low-income residence programs, urban community programs, and camping programs. For information contact Brethren in Christ Missions, 500 South Angle Street, Route 1, Mount Joy, PA 17552. Phone (717) 653-8067. Canadians may contact Brethren in Christ Missions, 2519 Stevensville Road, Stevensville, Ontario L0S 1J0. Phone (416) 382-3144.

*Mennonite Central Committee (MCC)*

MCC seeks persons who are committed to the lordship of Jesus Christ and the biblical principles of love, service, and nonresistance and have skills in one of the following technical areas: education, agriculture, health, social services, and economic and technical development. Canadian programs focus on offender ministries, native concerns, and handicapped services. Canadians should apply to Mennonite Central Committee Canada, 201-1483 Pembina Highway, Winnipeg, Manitoba R3T 2C8. Phone (204) 475-3550. American should apply to Mennonite Central Committee, 21 South 12th Street, Akron, PA 17501. Phone (717) 859-1151.

*Brethren Volunteer Service*

"Sharing God's love through acts of service" is a phrase that has been used to capture the essence and spirit of Brethren Volunteer Service. BVS has existed since 1948 through the sponsorship of the Church of the Brethren. The program challenges persons to give of their time and talents in service towards three scripturally inspired goals: advocating justice, peacemaking, and serving basic human needs. Volunteers 18 years of age and older serve in a variety of settings in the United States and overseas in education, community development, health care, agriculture, youth ministry, and many others. Updated information is available free from Brethren Volunteer Service, 1451 Dundee Ave., Elgin, IL 60120. Phone (312) 742-5100.